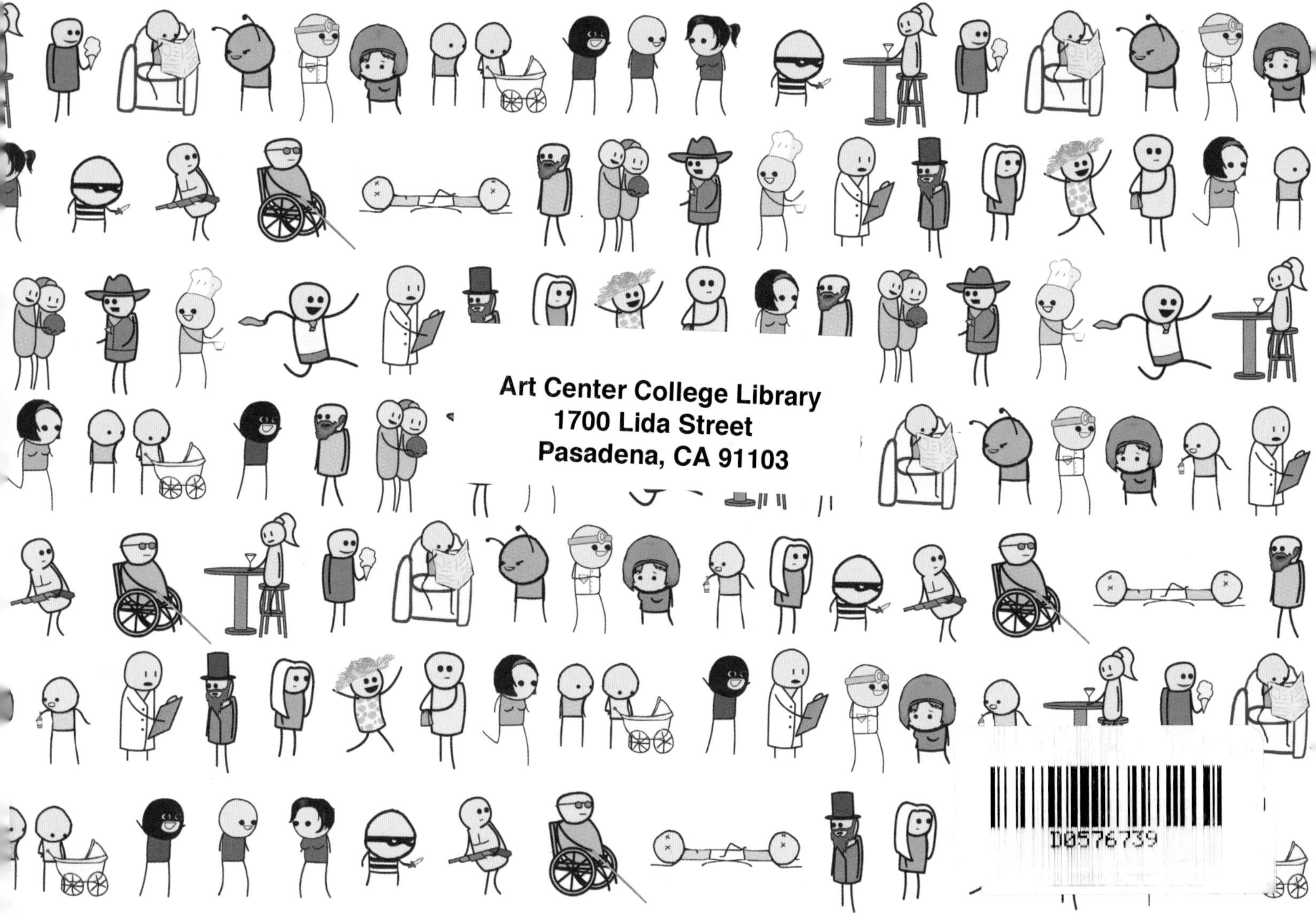

CYANIDE & HAPPINESS

Kris, Rob, Matt, & Dave

HarperCollins*Publishers*

HarperCollins*Publishers*
77—85 Fulham Palace Road,
Hammersmith, London W6 8JB
www.harpercollins.co.uk

First published by HarperCollins*Publishers* 2009

© 2009 Kris Wilson, Rob DenBleyker, Matt Melvin, and Dave McElfatrick

Cover illustration © 2009 Kris Wilson

10 9 8 7 6 5 4 3 2 1

A catalogue record of this book is available from the British Library

ISBN 978-0-00-731886-5

Printed and bound in China by Leo Paper Products Limited

DEDICATED TO GEFF

Many thanks to Jeannine Dillon for her ridiculous amount of patience,
Tom Fulp for giving us a launching pad to make our hobby a career,
Maddox and the Tomorrow's Nobody guys for graciously letting us crash their
Comic Con booth, our friends and family for their never-ending support and
of course our fans for being so amazing.

Dear Reader,

If you picked up this book, congratulations. You've taken the first step toward making us wealthy.

For those of you who are already Cyanide & Happiness readers, what you're holding in your hands is a collection of what we *think* is some of our best work. In addition, we've made thirty brand new, never-before-seen, "too hot for the Internet" comics. You're probably flipping to them now (pp127).

And of course, for those of you who've never heard of Cyanide & Happiness, boy are you in for a surprise! What follows is a hand-picked collection from the daily online comic run by four dudes from all over the world. That's right, we don't even work together. We didn't even meet until two years ago, though we've been drawing the comic for four years and running. We were bound not by cultures and borders, but by our love for putting cute characters into awful, awful situations.

That's another thing. These comics get pretty crazy. If you're younger than 15 or older than 50 there is an 87% chance something in this book will offend you. Our team of humour analysts has confirmed this.

So carry on, enjoy yourself. You've been warned. These aren't your grandma's Sunday funnies, but I think that's why we like them. Your grandma's sort of a bitch.

-Kris, Rob, Matt & Dave

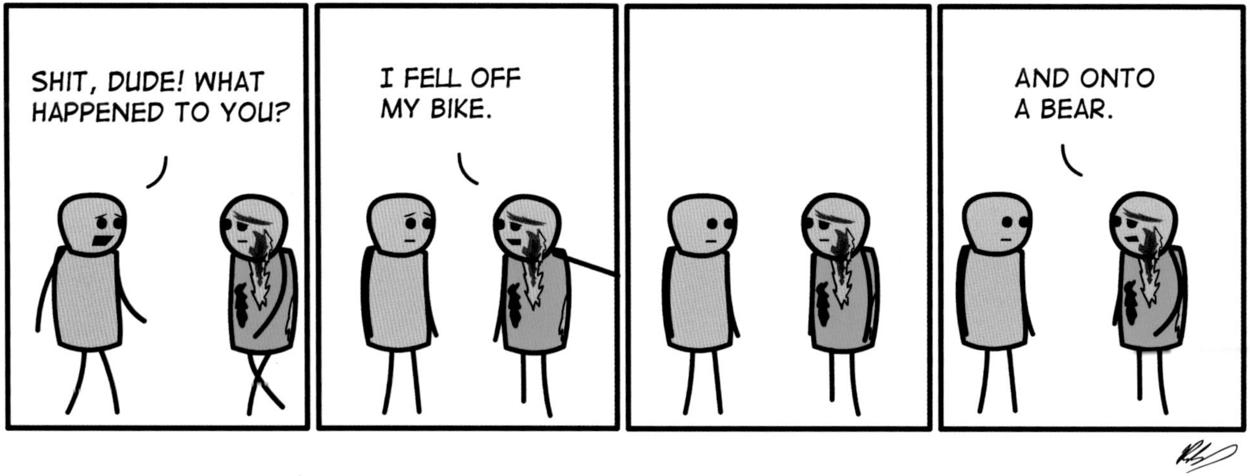
SHIT, DUDE! WHAT HAPPENED TO YOU?
I FELL OFF MY BIKE.
AND ONTO A BEAR.

CHARLES, I'VE TOLD YOU TO FIX THAT LEAK FOR MONTHS NOW.
WHAT AM I, A PLUMBER? I DON'T EVEN KNOW HOW!
CAN'T YOU JUST USE DUCT TAPE?
IT'S WORTH A SHOT

AWW. YOUR BABY IS GROWING SO FAST
I KNOW! IT SAID ITS FIRST WORDS LAST WEEK
SOON IT WILL BE WALKING AROUND...
IT WILL SMILE AND PLAY GAMES AND BE HAPPY
AND THEN IT WILL DIE
KW '06

I THOUGHT I TOLD YOU NOT TO DRAW ON THE WALLS!
KW '06

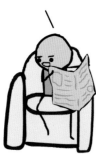

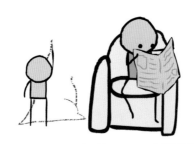

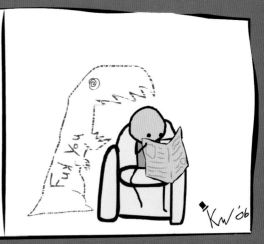

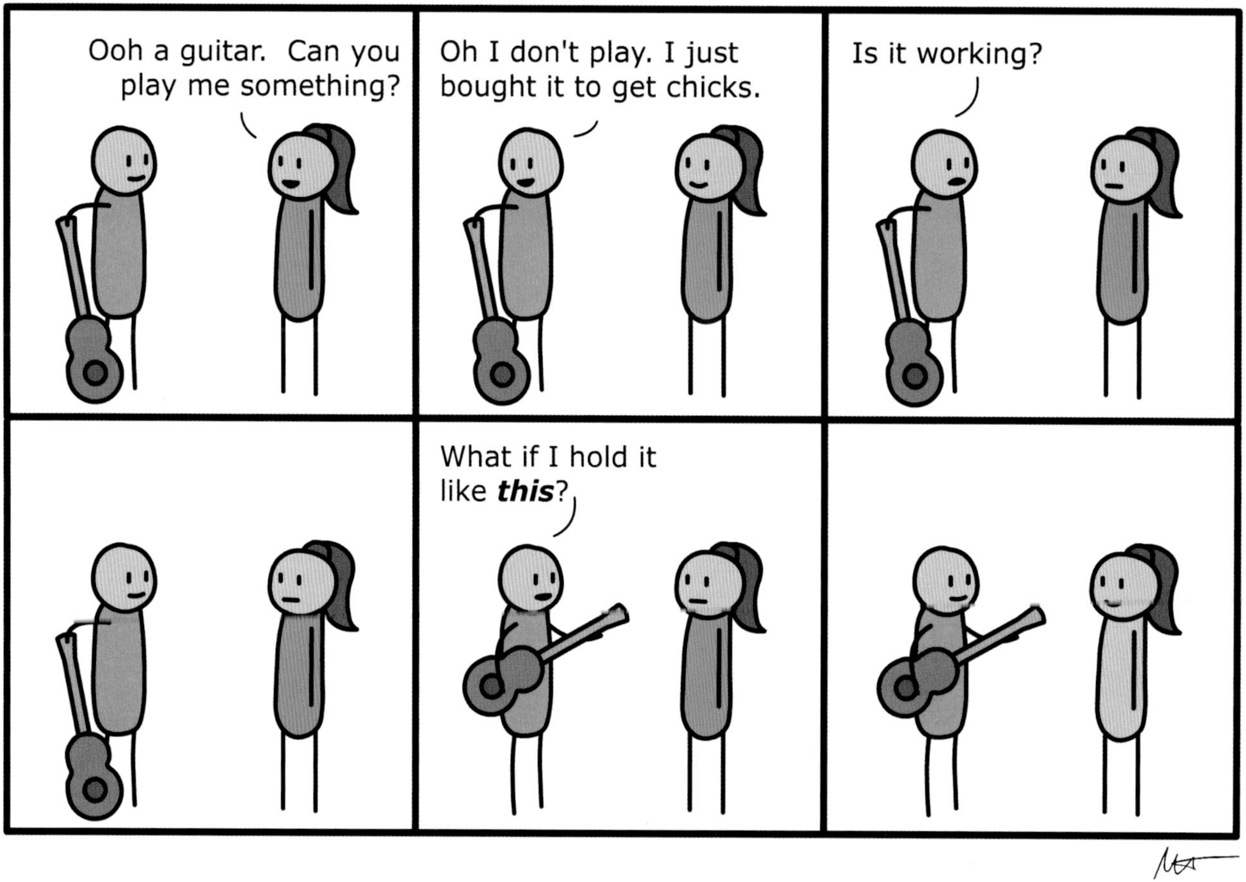
Ooh a guitar. Can you play me something?
Oh I don't play. I just bought it to get chicks.
Is it working?
What if I hold it like ***this***?

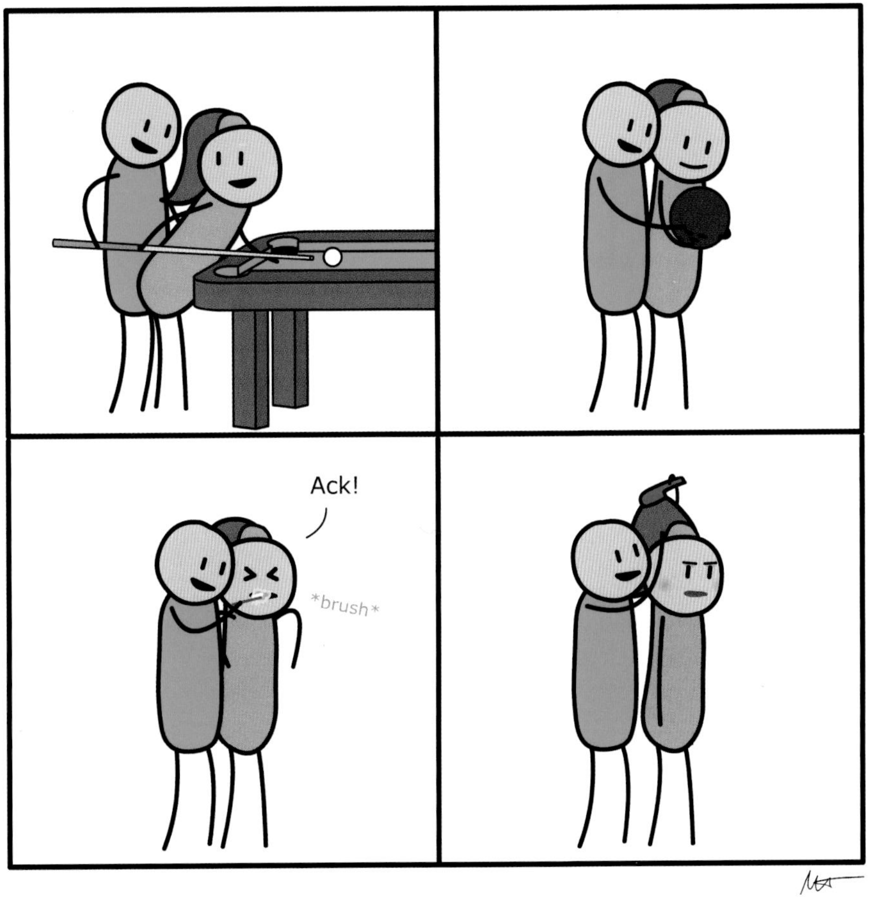
Ack!
brush

SO, CAN I HAVE YOUR NUMBER?
SURE!
CRACK!!
DAVE

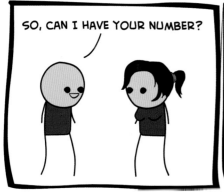

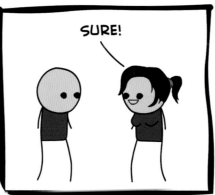

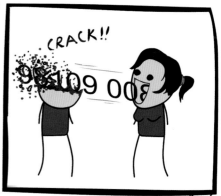

PENTHOUSE
DAVE

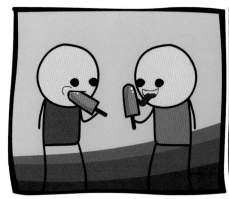

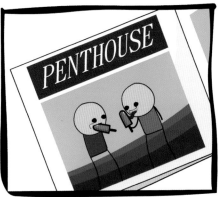

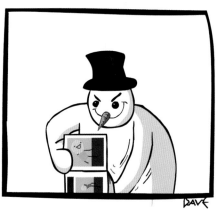

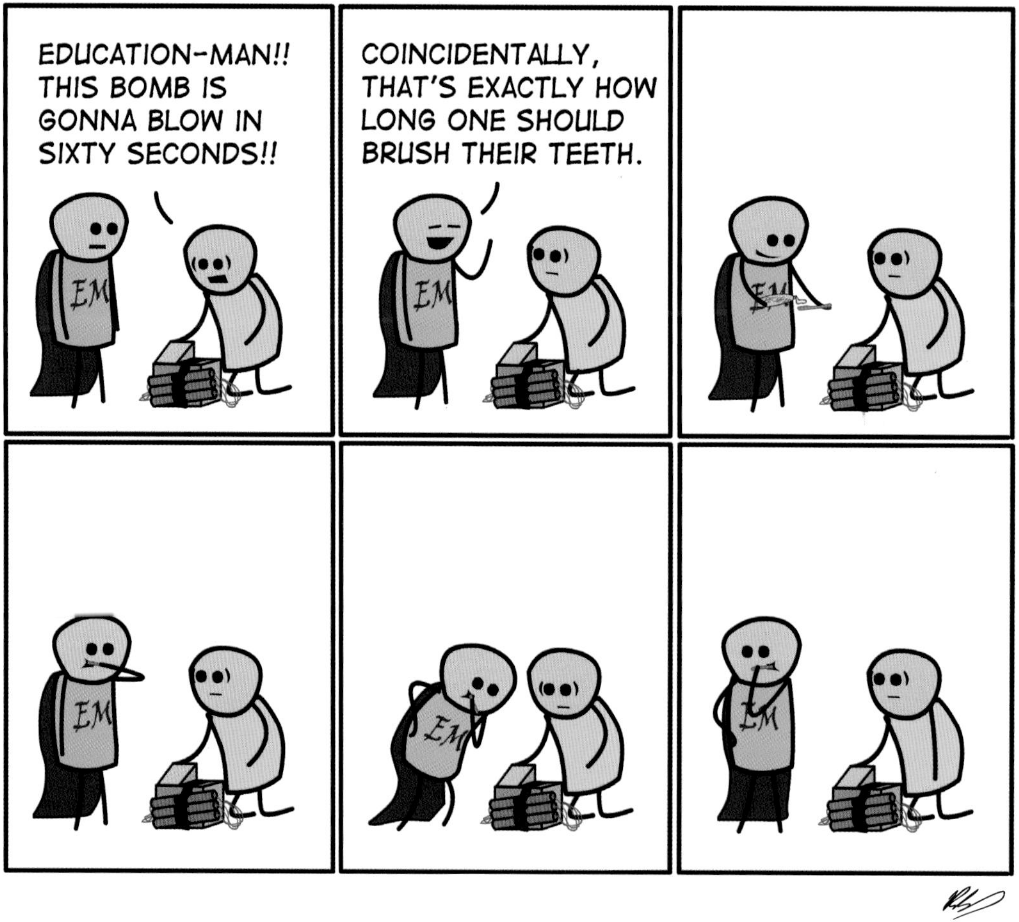
EDUCATION-MAN!! THIS BOMB IS GONNA BLOW IN SIXTY SECONDS!!
COINCIDENTALLY, THAT'S EXACTLY HOW LONG ONE SHOULD BRUSH THEIR TEETH.
EM

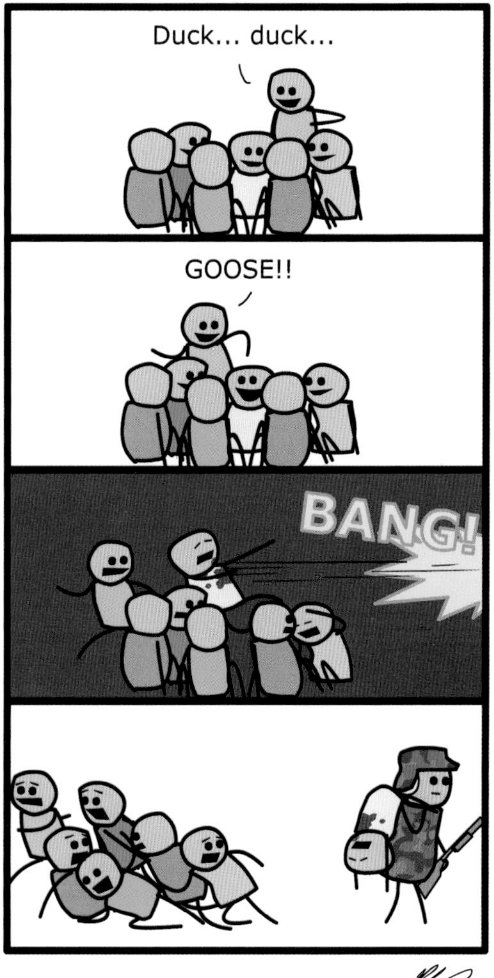
Duck... duck...
GOOSE!!
BANG!

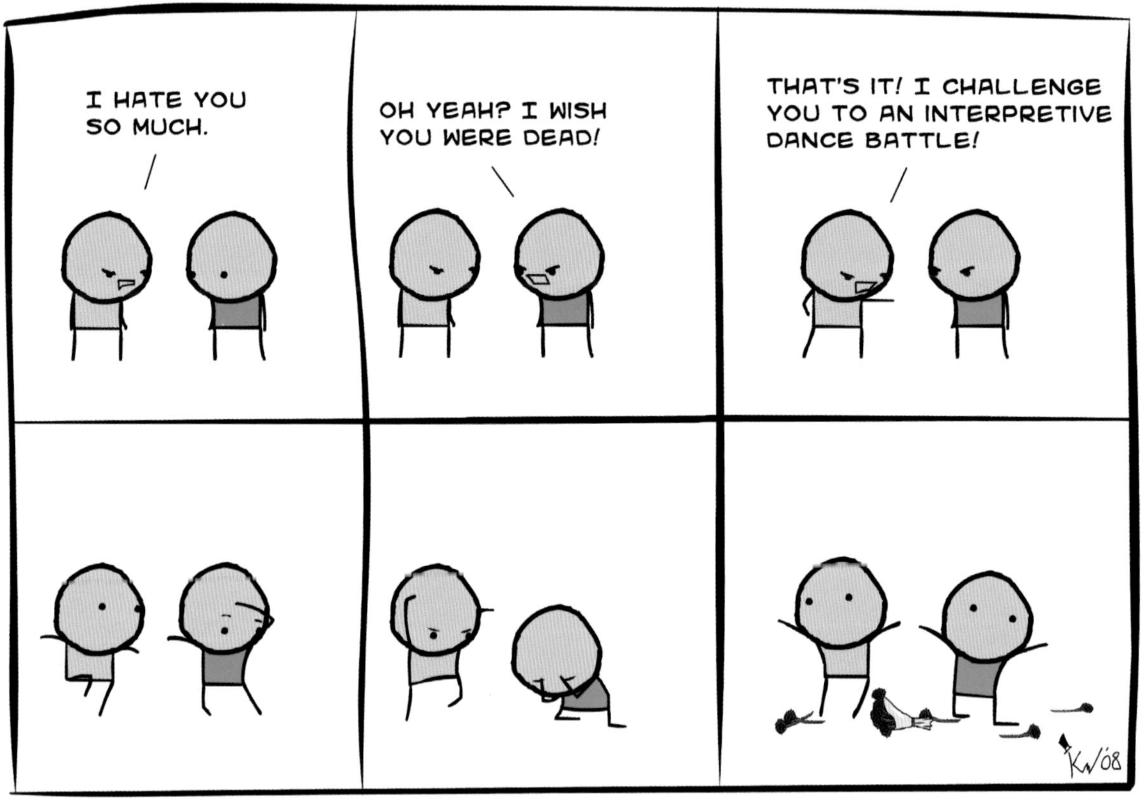
I HATE YOU SO MUCH.
OH YEAH? I WISH YOU WERE DEAD!
THAT'S IT! I CHALLENGE YOU TO AN INTERPRETIVE DANCE BATTLE!
KW'08

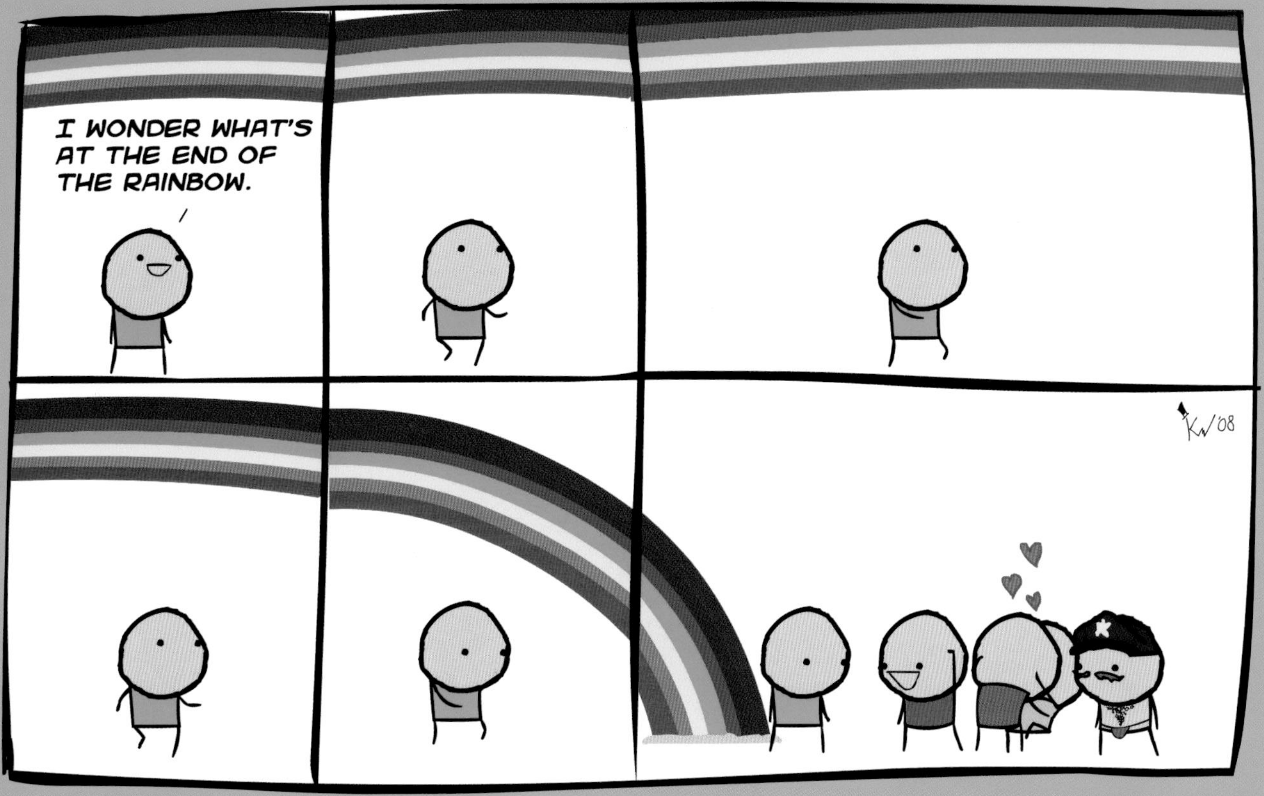
I WONDER WHAT'S AT THE END OF THE RAINBOW.
KW '08

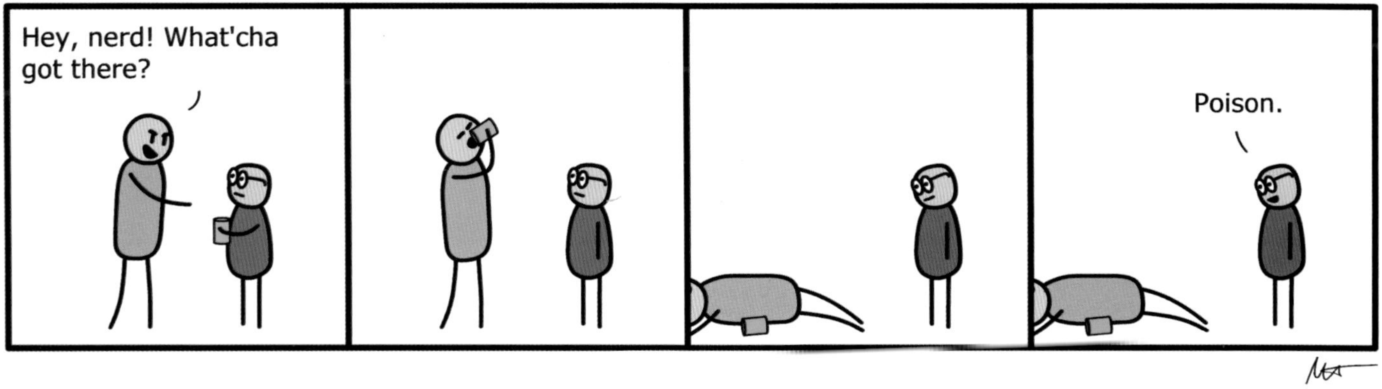
Hey, nerd! What'cha got there?
Poison.

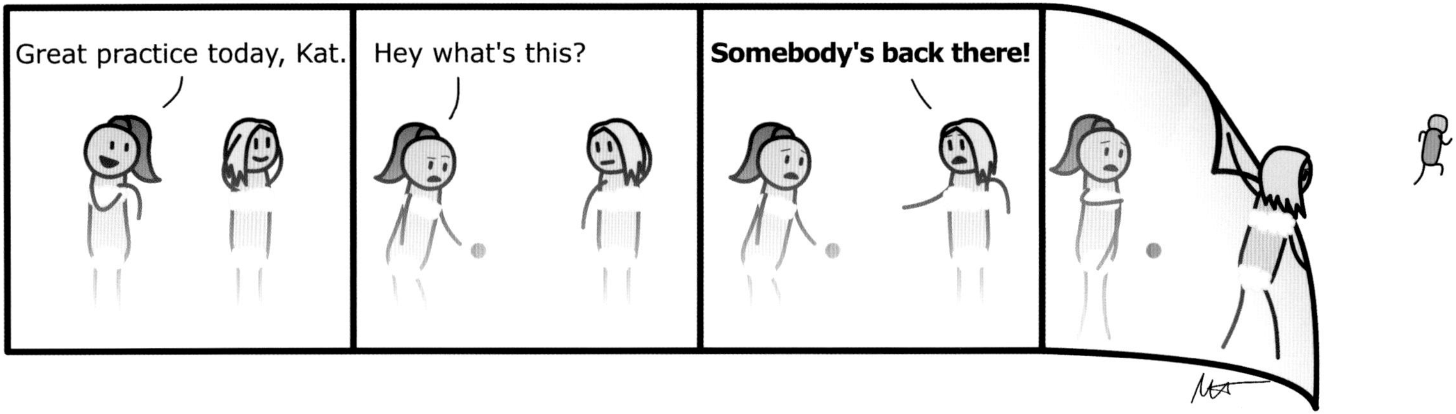
Great practice today, Kat.
Hey what's this?
Somebody's back there!

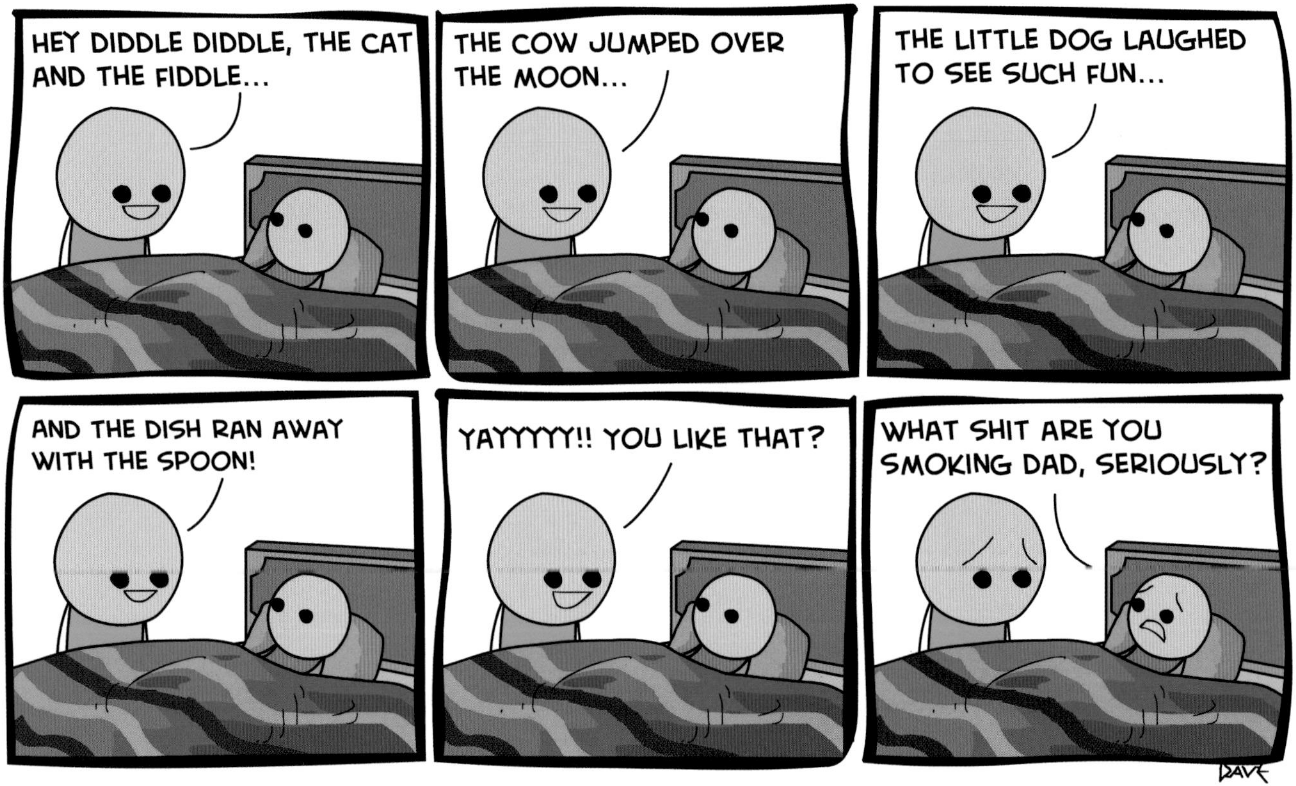
HEY DIDDLE DIDDLE, THE CAT AND THE FIDDLE...
THE COW JUMPED OVER THE MOON...
THE LITTLE DOG LAUGHED TO SEE SUCH FUN...
AND THE DISH RAN AWAY WITH THE SPOON!
YAYYYYY!! YOU LIKE THAT?
WHAT SHIT ARE YOU SMOKING DAD, SERIOUSLY?
DAVE

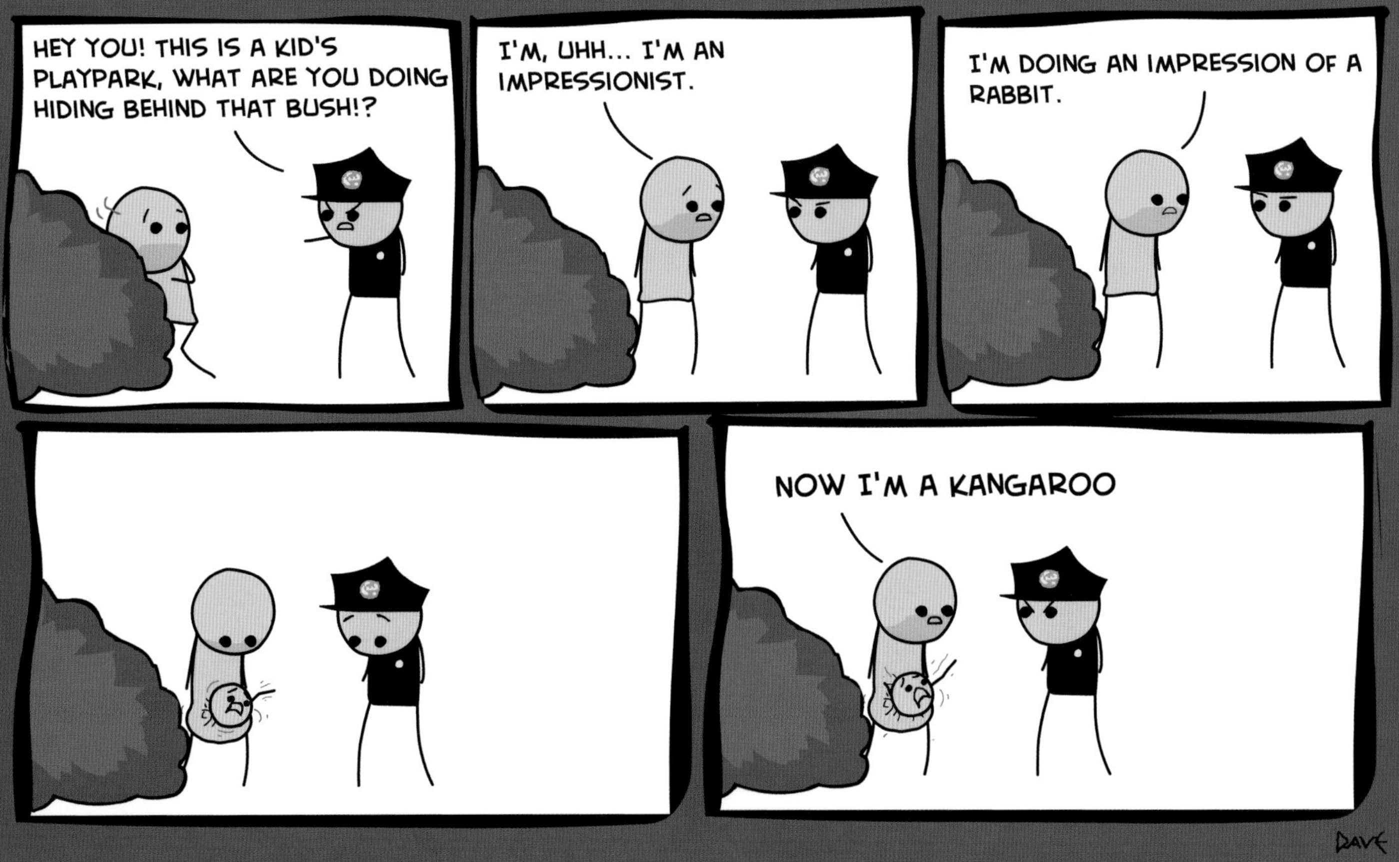
HEY YOU! THIS IS A KID'S PLAYPARK, WHAT ARE YOU DOING HIDING BEHIND THAT BUSH!?
I'M, UHH... I'M AN IMPRESSIONIST.
I'M DOING AN IMPRESSION OF A RABBIT.
NOW I'M A KANGAROO
DAVE

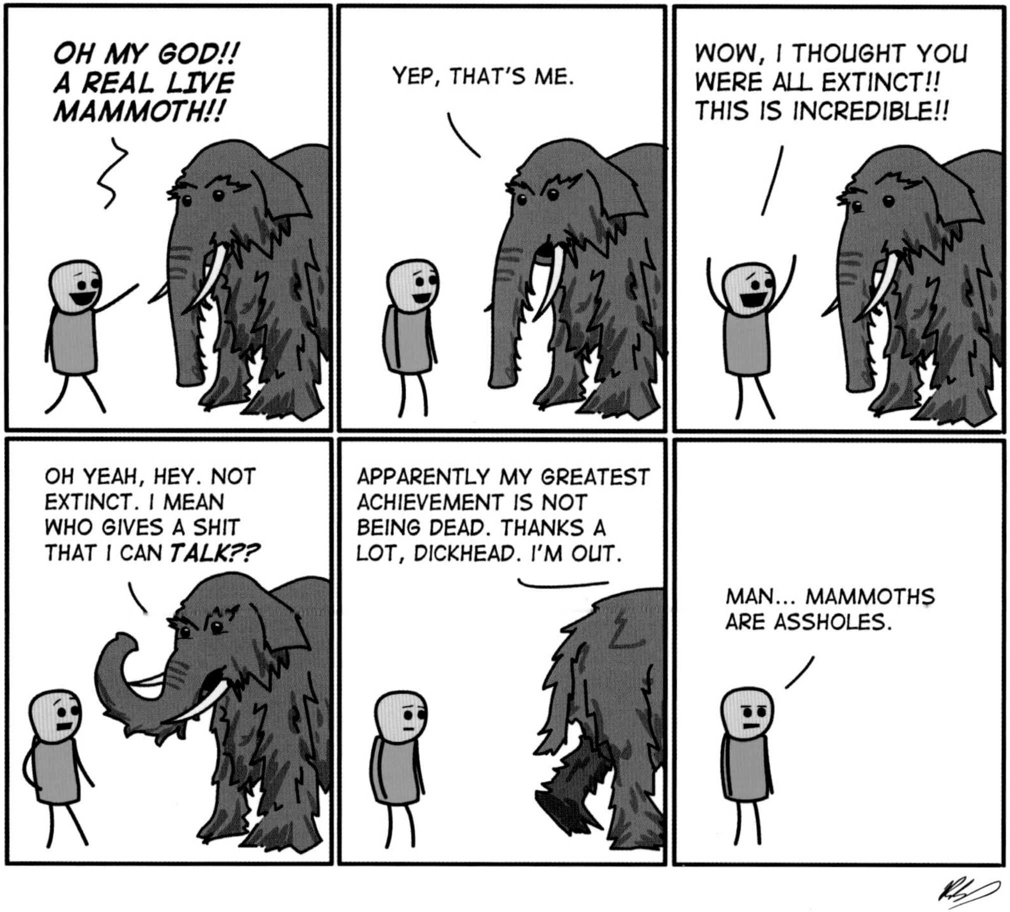
OH MY GOD!! A REAL LIVE MAMMOTH!!
YEP, THAT'S ME.
WOW, I THOUGHT YOU WERE ALL EXTINCT!! THIS IS INCREDIBLE!!
OH YEAH, HEY. NOT EXTINCT. I MEAN WHO GIVES A SHIT THAT I CAN TALK??
APPARENTLY MY GREATEST ACHIEVEMENT IS NOT BEING DEAD. THANKS A LOT, DICKHEAD. I'M OUT.
MAN... MAMMOTHS ARE ASSHOLES.

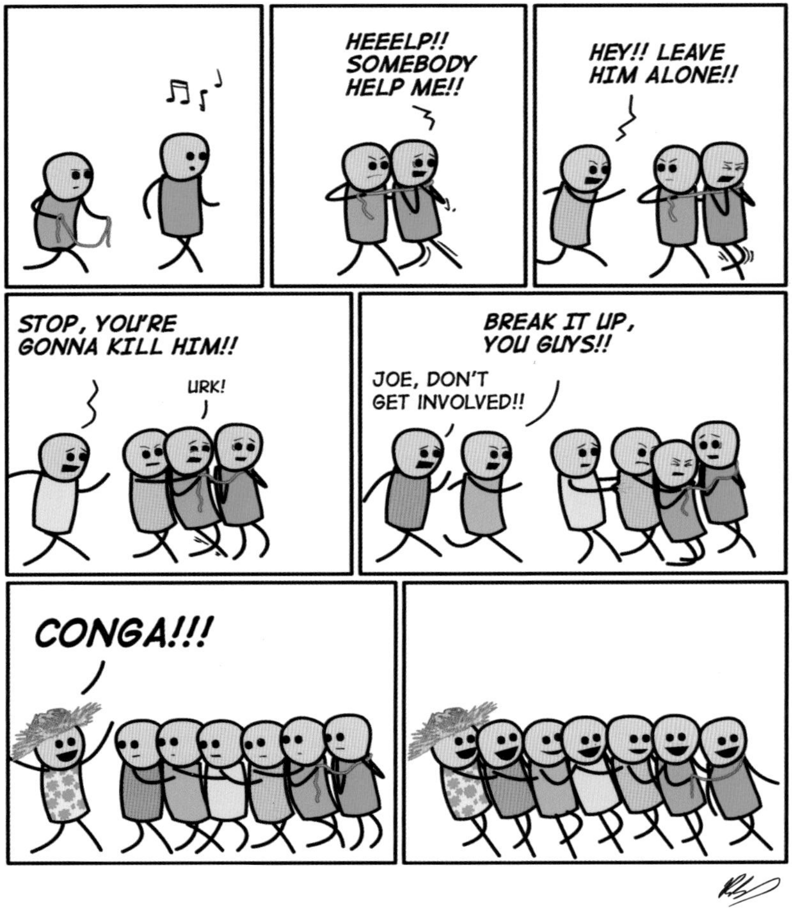
HEEELP!! SOMEBODY HELP ME!!
HEY!! LEAVE HIM ALONE!!
STOP, YOU'RE GONNA KILL HIM!!
URK!
BREAK IT UP, YOU GUYS!!
JOE, DON'T GET INVOLVED!!
CONGA!!!

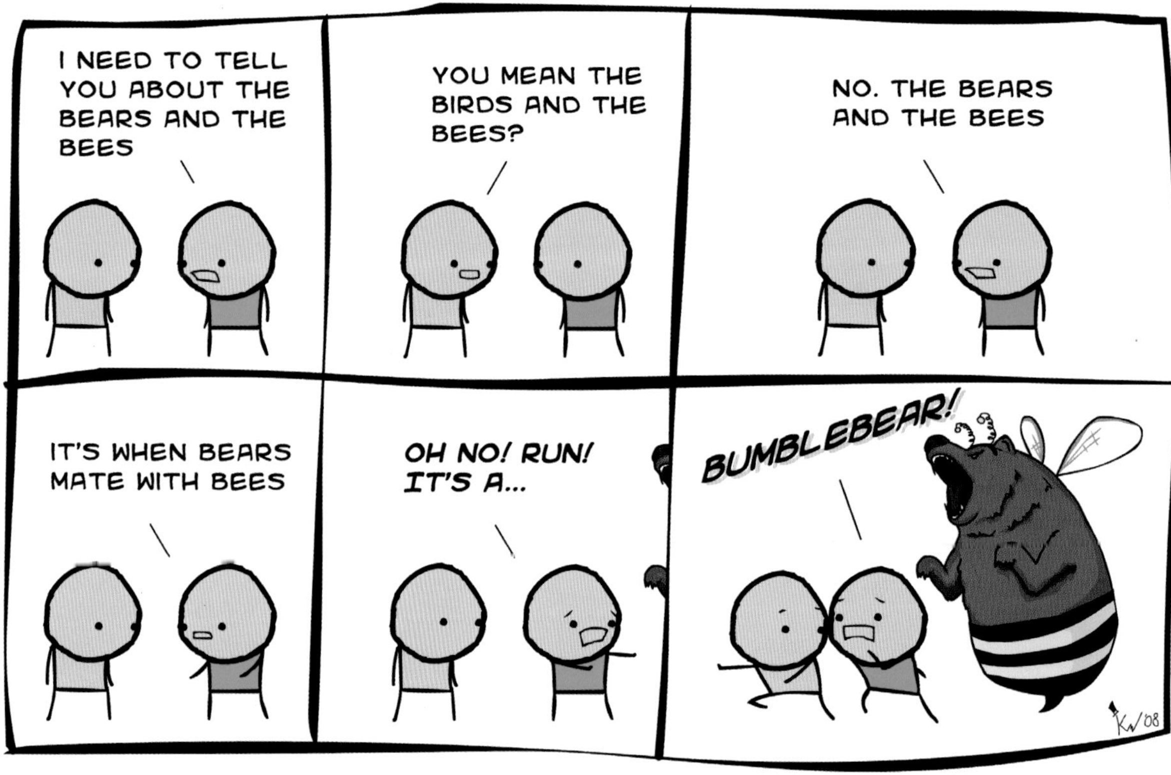
I NEED TO TELL YOU ABOUT THE BEARS AND THE BEES
YOU MEAN THE BIRDS AND THE BEES?
NO. THE BEARS AND THE BEES
IT'S WHEN BEARS MATE WITH BEES
OH NO! RUN! IT'S A...
BUMBLEBEAR!
KW '08

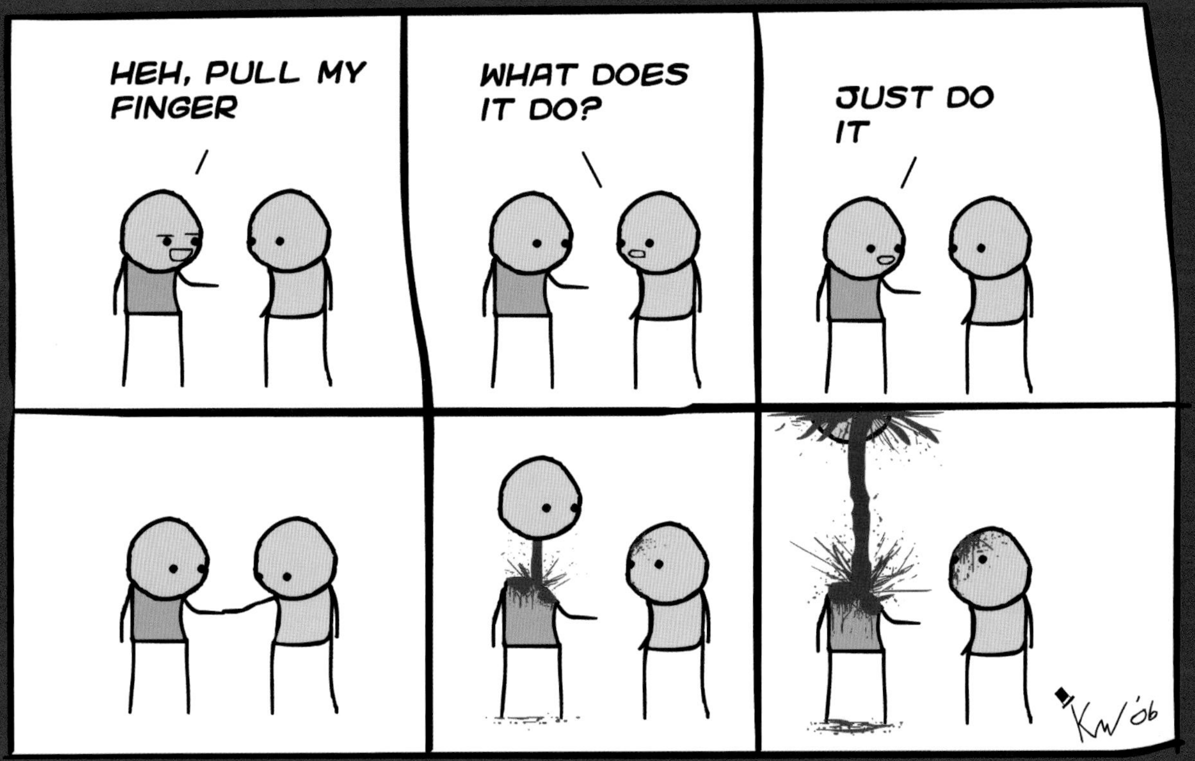
HEH, PULL MY FINGER
WHAT DOES IT DO?
JUST DO IT
KW '06

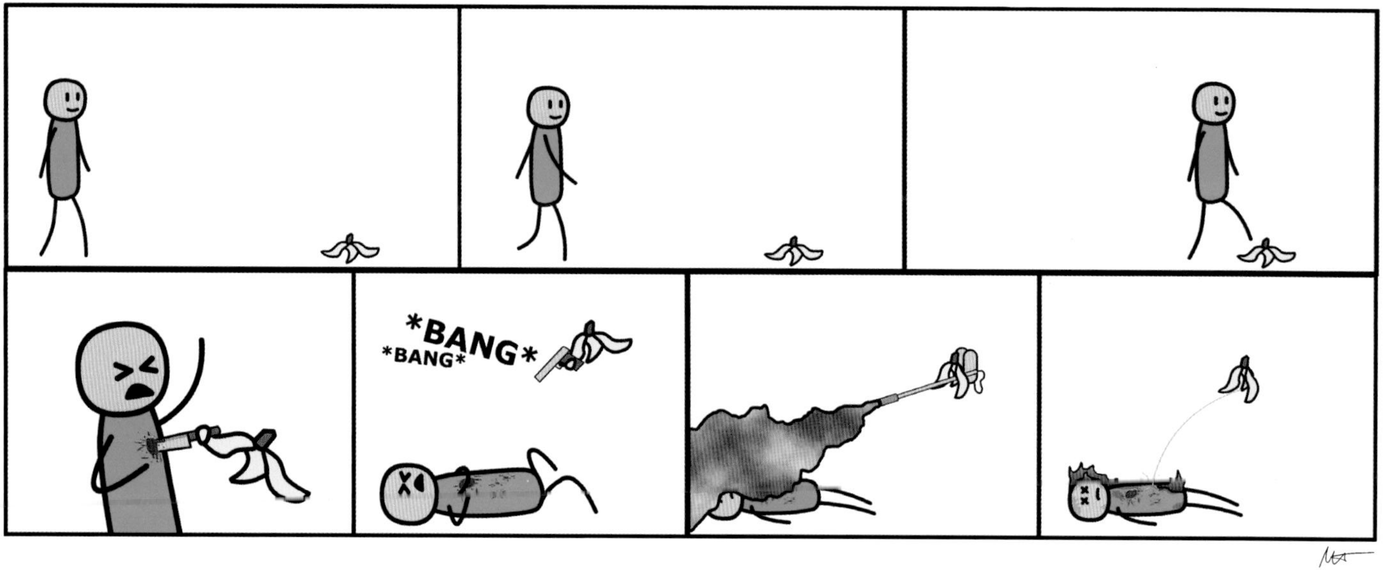
BANG
BANG

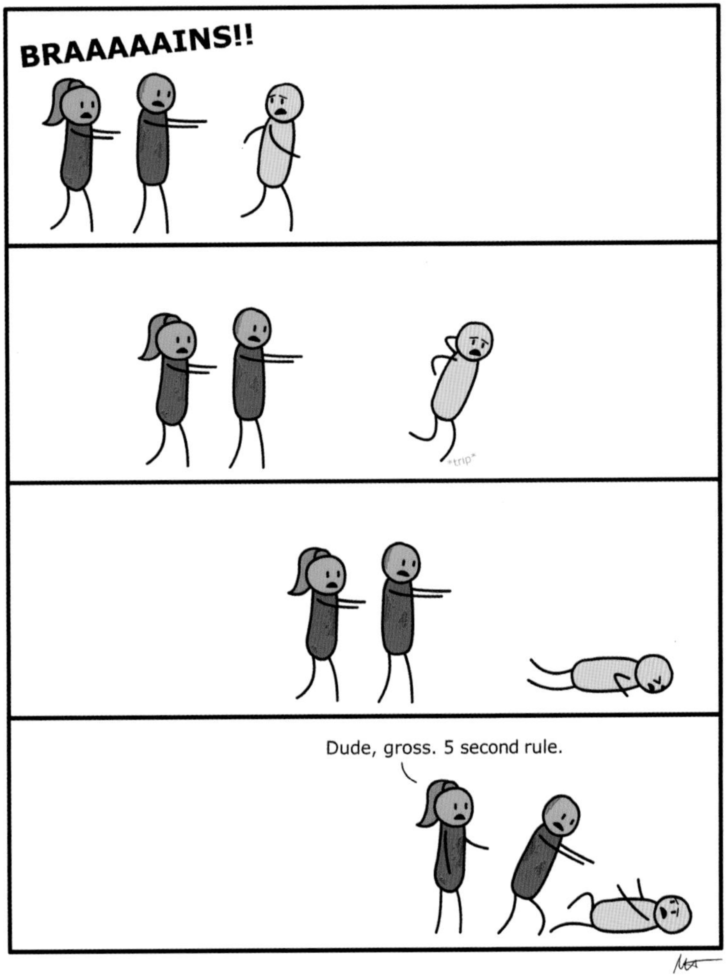
BRAAAAAINS!!
trip
Dude, gross. 5 second rule.

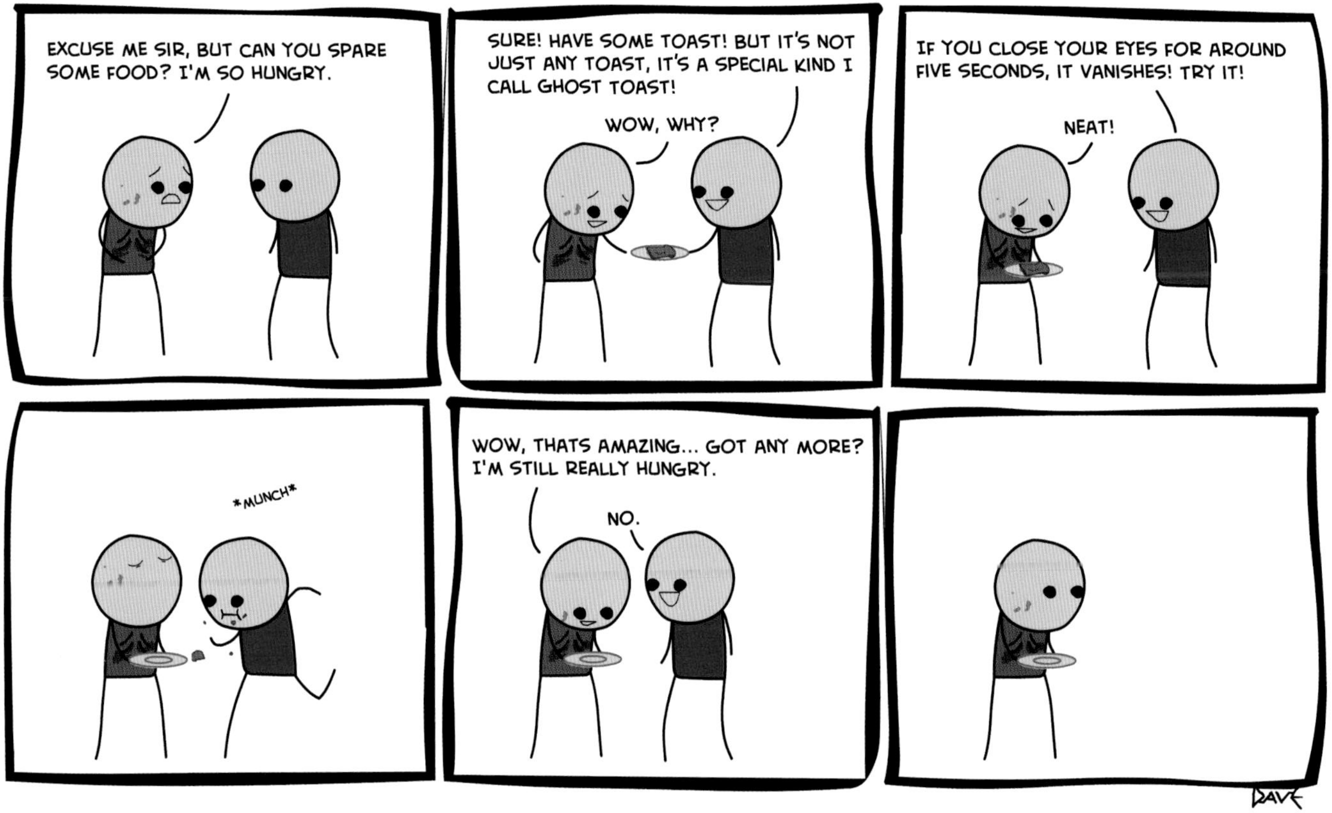
EXCUSE ME SIR, BUT CAN YOU SPARE SOME FOOD? I'M SO HUNGRY.
SURE! HAVE SOME TOAST! BUT IT'S NOT JUST ANY TOAST, IT'S A SPECIAL KIND I CALL GHOST TOAST!
WOW, WHY?
IF YOU CLOSE YOUR EYES FOR AROUND FIVE SECONDS, IT VANISHES! TRY IT!
NEAT!
MUNCH
WOW, THATS AMAZING... GOT ANY MORE? I'M STILL REALLY HUNGRY.
NO.
DAVE

WHAT'S WITH ALL THE COLOURED SQUARES?
OH SHI...
AAAARRRGGHH!!
DAVE

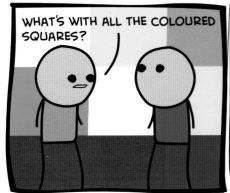

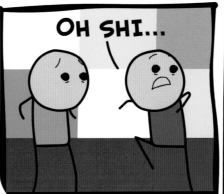

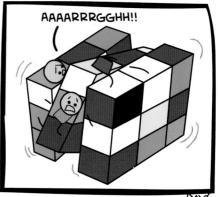

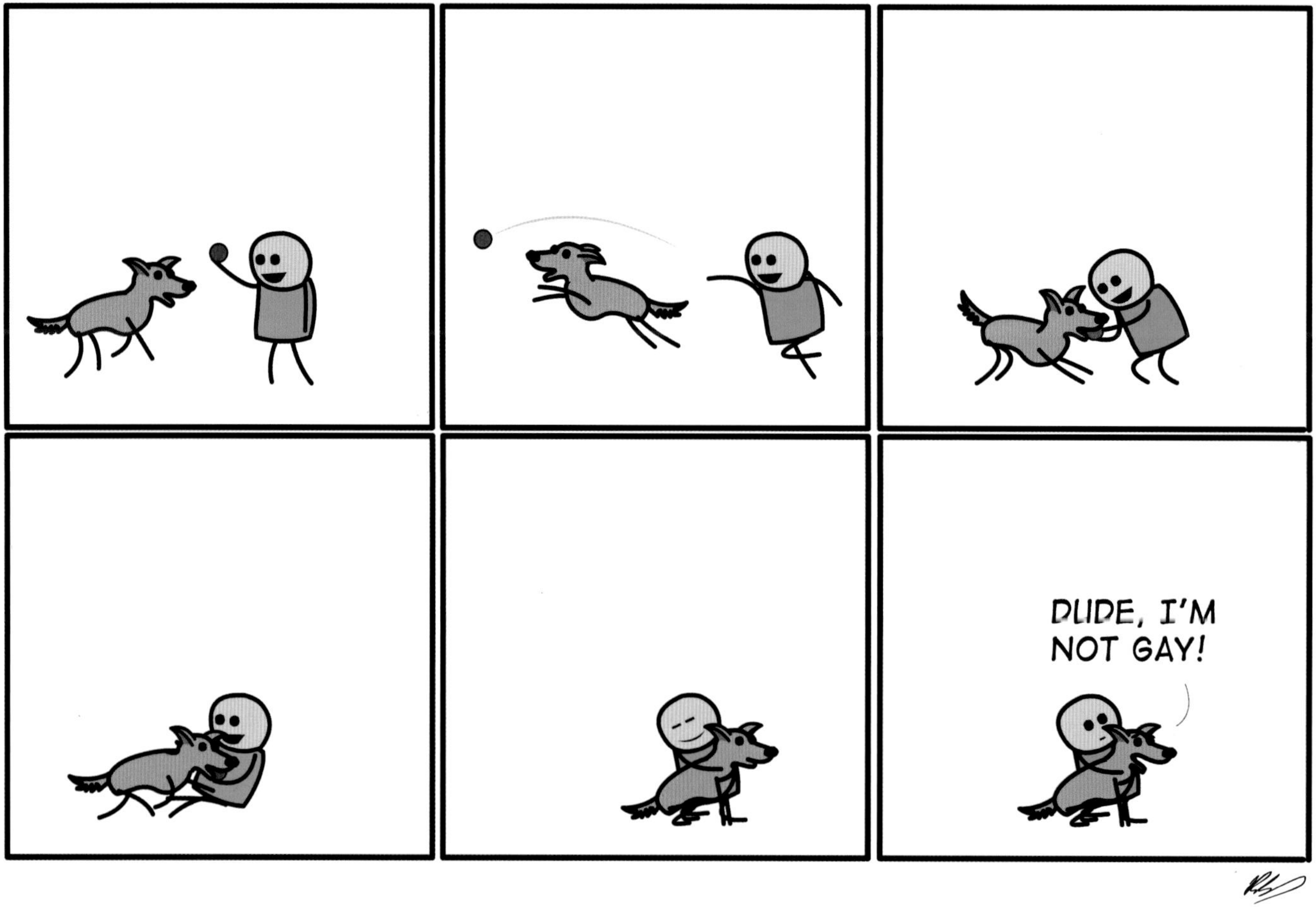
DUDE, I'M
NOT GAY!

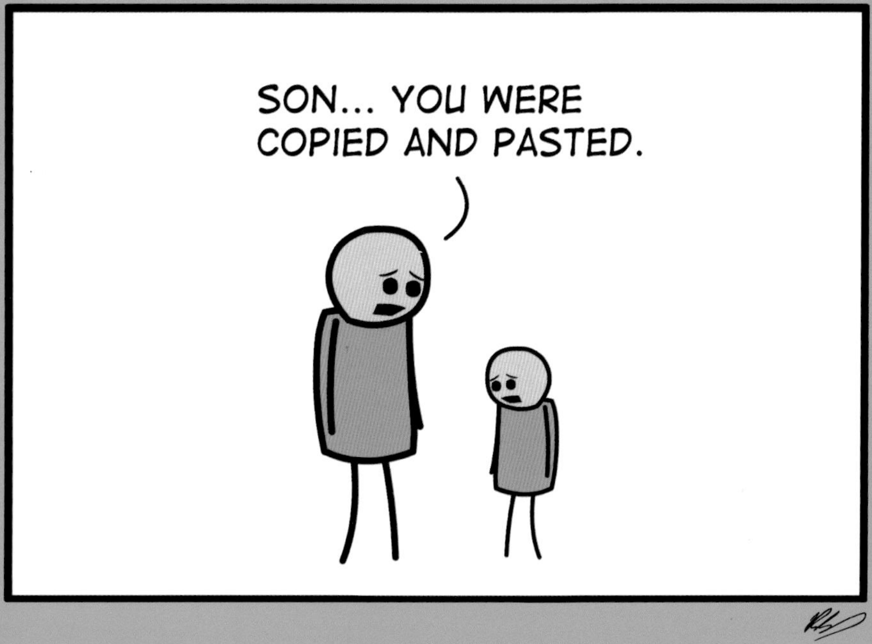
SON... YOU WERE COPIED AND PASTED.

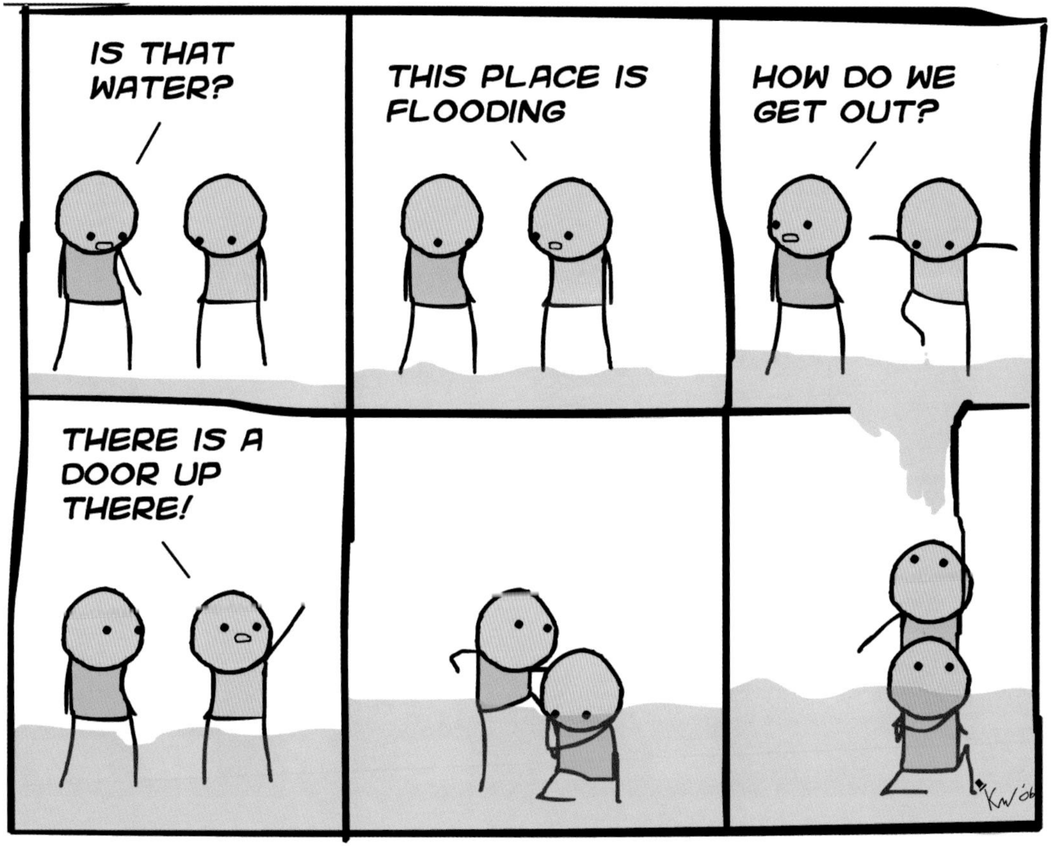
IS THAT WATER?
THIS PLACE IS FLOODING
HOW DO WE GET OUT?
THERE IS A DOOR UP THERE!
KW '06

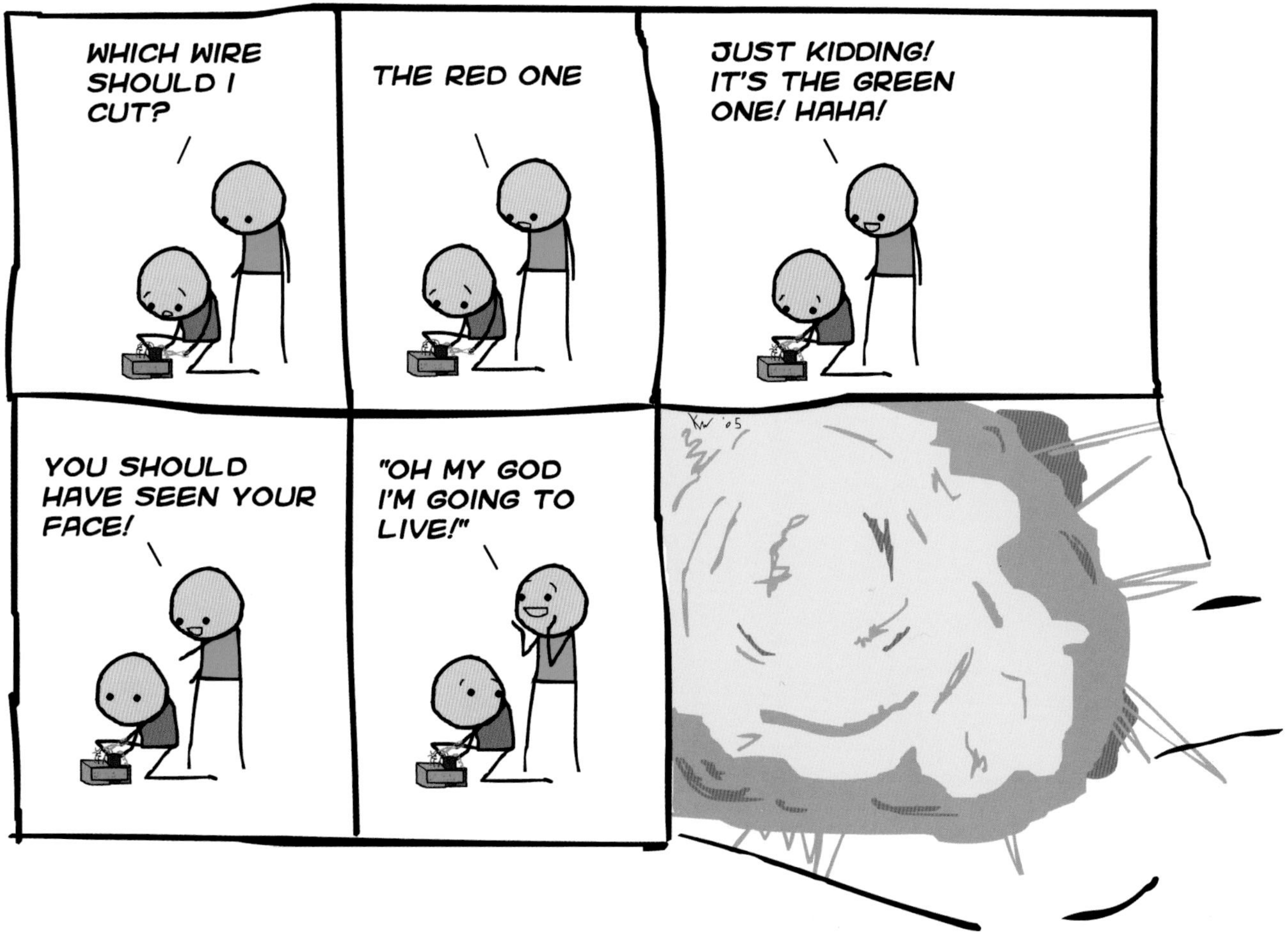
WHICH WIRE SHOULD I CUT?
THE RED ONE
JUST KIDDING! IT'S THE GREEN ONE! HAHA!
YOU SHOULD HAVE SEEN YOUR FACE!
"OH MY GOD I'M GOING TO LIVE!"

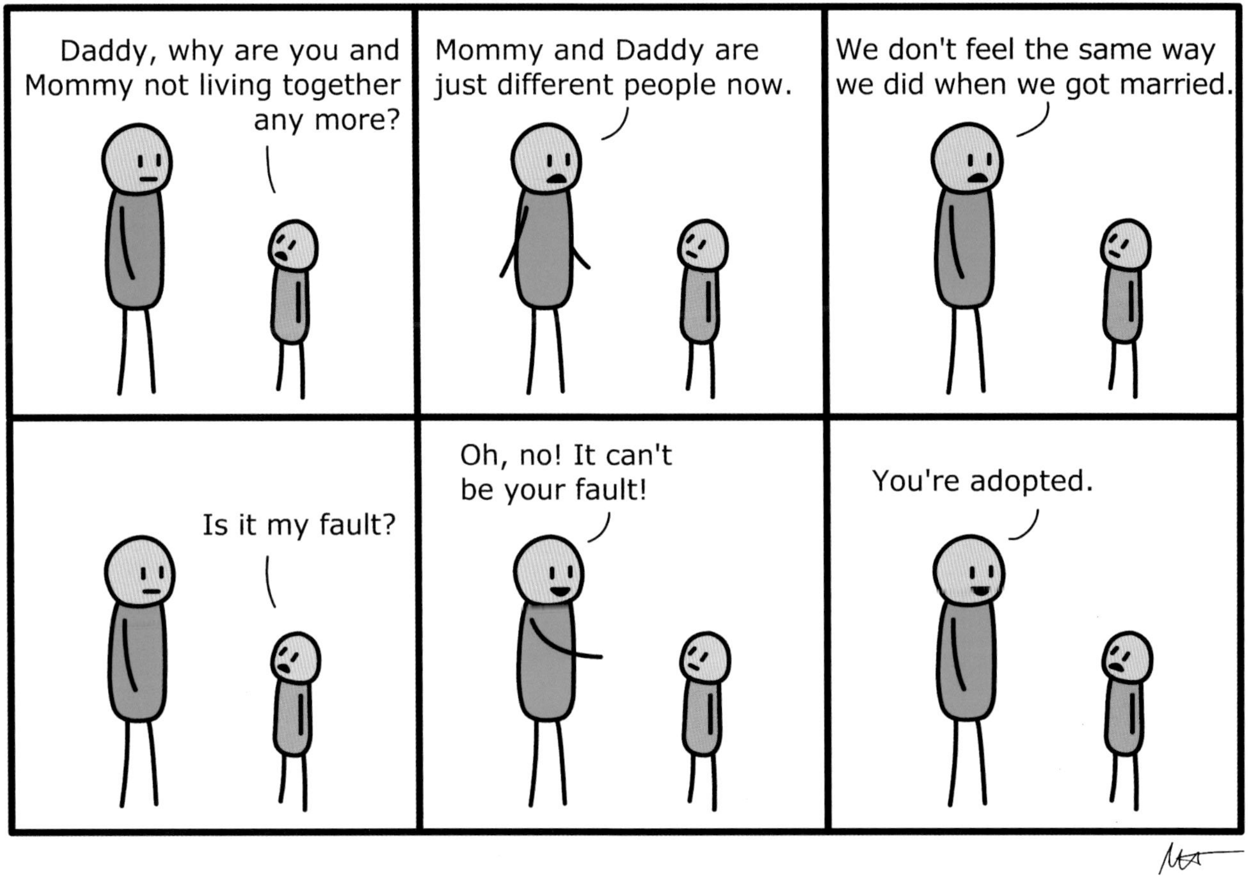
Daddy, why are you and Mommy not living together any more?
Mommy and Daddy are just different people now.
We don't feel the same way we did when we got married.
Is it my fault?
Oh, no! It can't be your fault!
You're adopted.

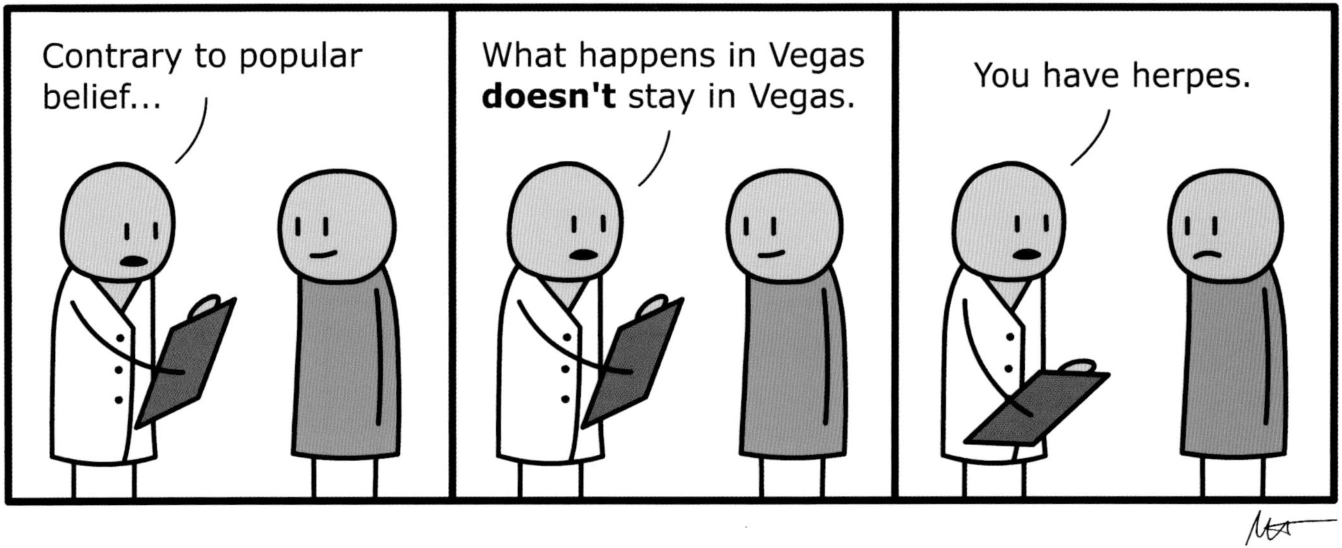
Contrary to popular belief...
What happens in Vegas **doesn't** stay in Vegas.
You have herpes.

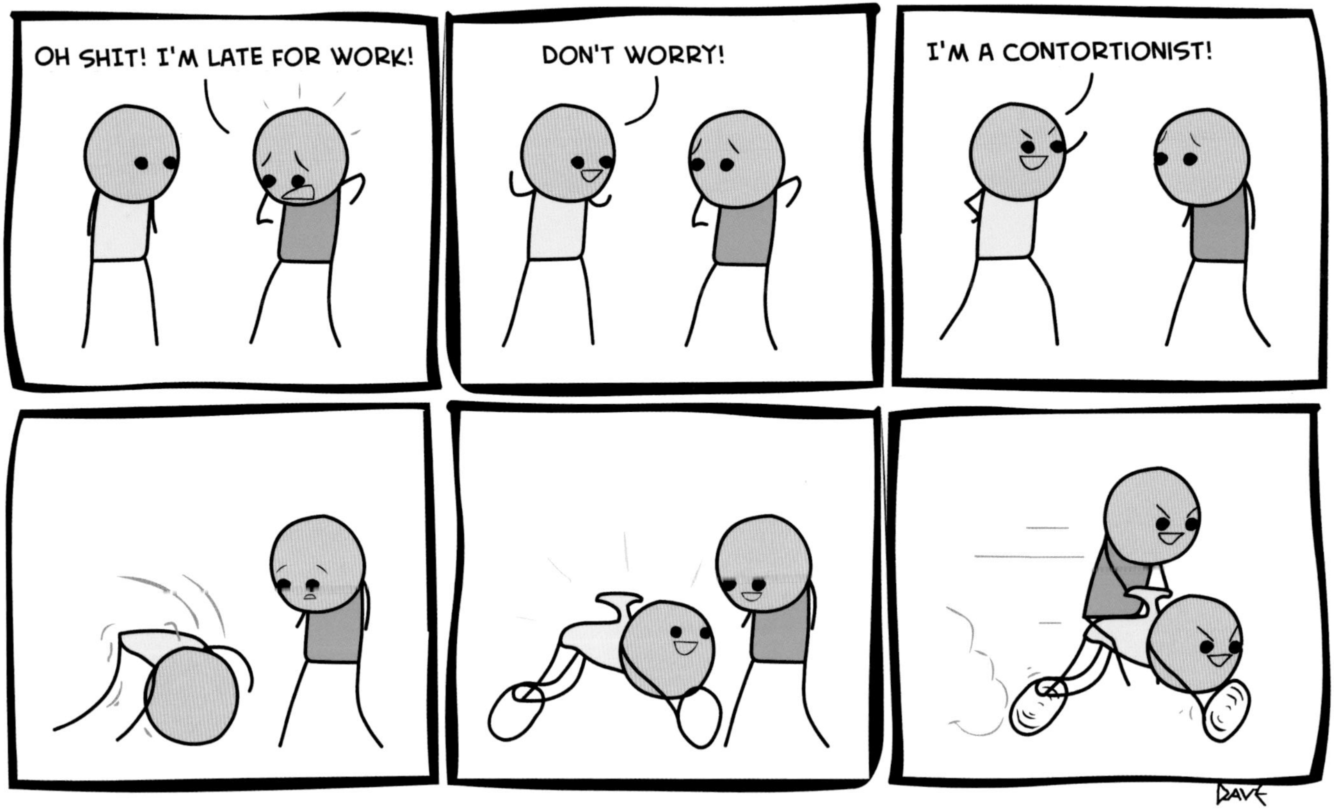
OH SHIT! I'M LATE FOR WORK!
DON'T WORRY!
I'M A CONTORTIONIST!
DAVE

SO I TOLD MARY HOW I FELT AND SHE SAID SHE FELT THE SAME BUT... OH, HANG ON DUDE, I THINK MY BATTERY'S DYING.
BEEOOWWW!!
DAVE

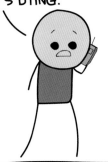

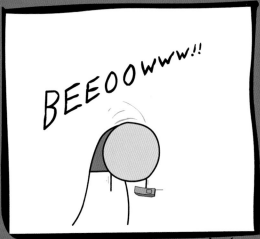

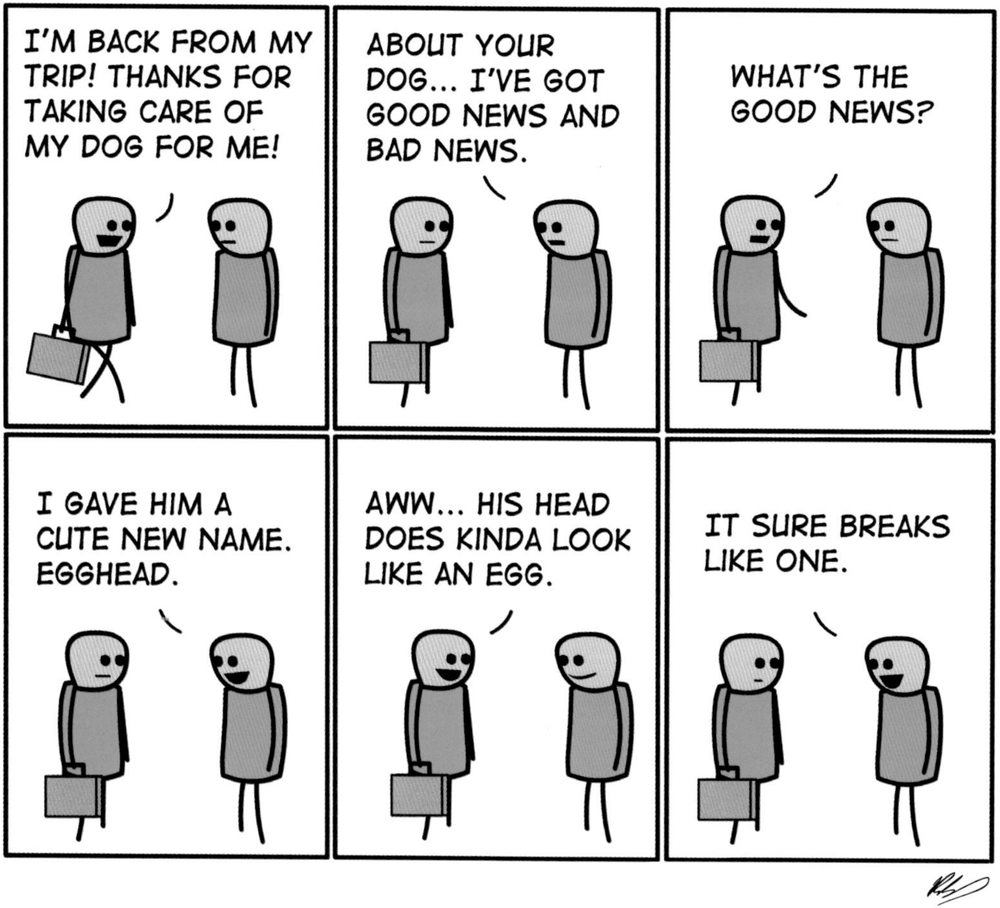
I'M BACK FROM MY TRIP! THANKS FOR TAKING CARE OF MY DOG FOR ME!
ABOUT YOUR DOG... I'VE GOT GOOD NEWS AND BAD NEWS.
WHAT'S THE GOOD NEWS?
I GAVE HIM A CUTE NEW NAME. EGGHEAD.
AWW... HIS HEAD DOES KINDA LOOK LIKE AN EGG.
IT SURE BREAKS LIKE ONE.

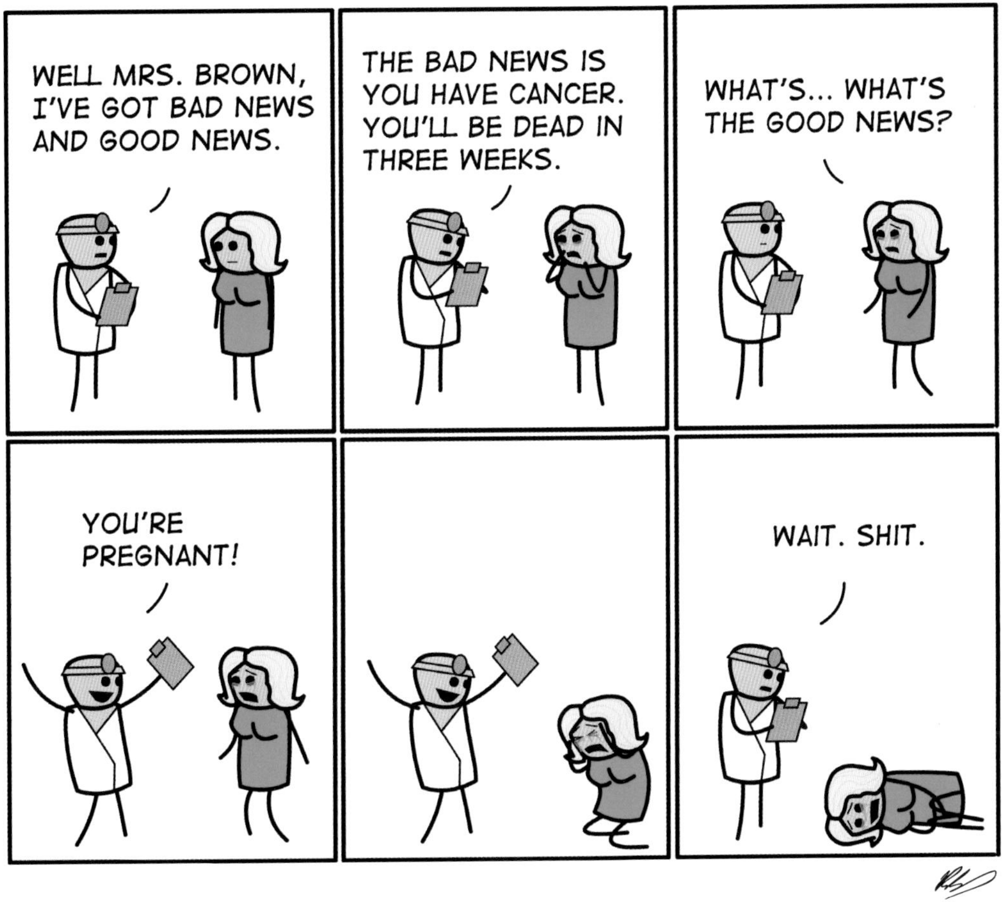
WELL MRS. BROWN, I'VE GOT BAD NEWS AND GOOD NEWS.
THE BAD NEWS IS YOU HAVE CANCER. YOU'LL BE DEAD IN THREE WEEKS.
WHAT'S... WHAT'S THE GOOD NEWS?
YOU'RE PREGNANT!
WAIT. SHIT.

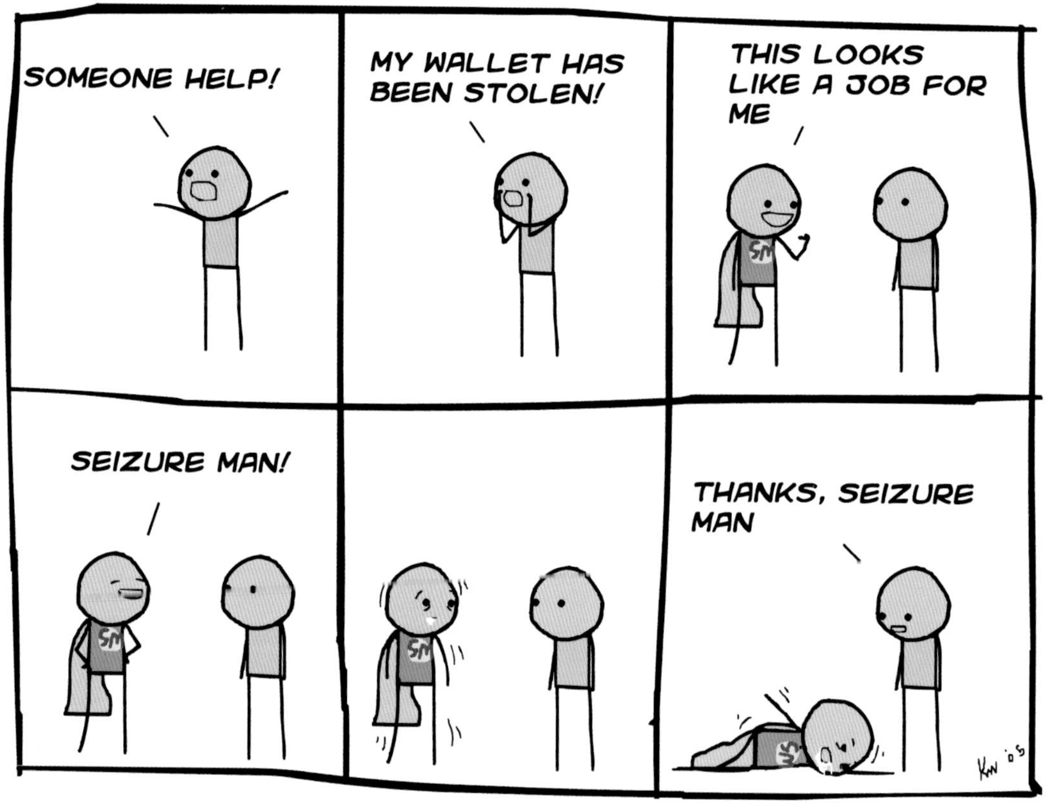
SOMEONE HELP!
MY WALLET HAS BEEN STOLEN!
THIS LOOKS LIKE A JOB FOR ME
SEIZURE MAN!
THANKS, SEIZURE MAN
KW '05

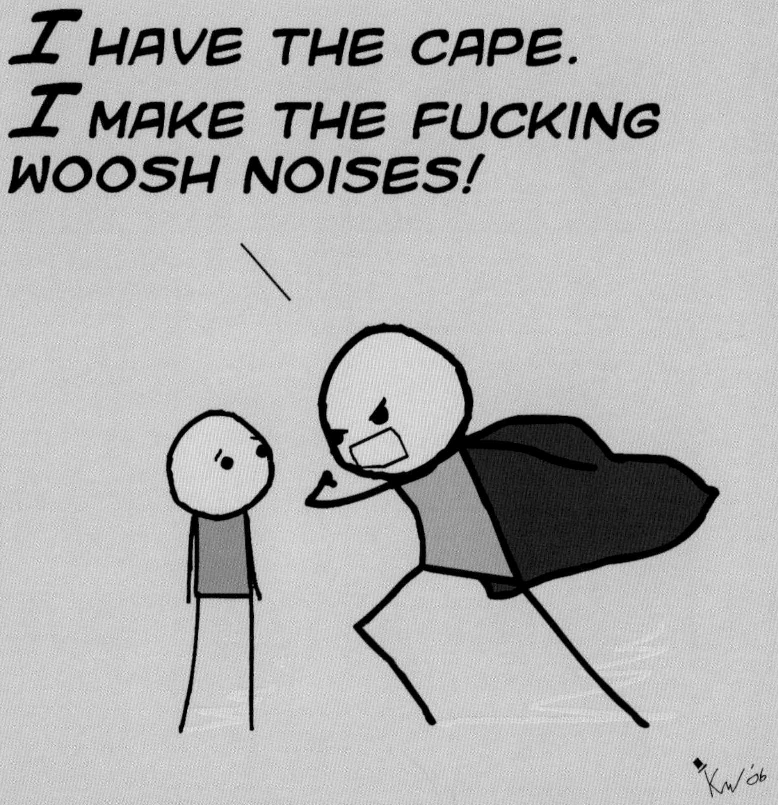
I HAVE THE CAPE.
I MAKE THE FUCKING WOOSH NOISES!
KW '06

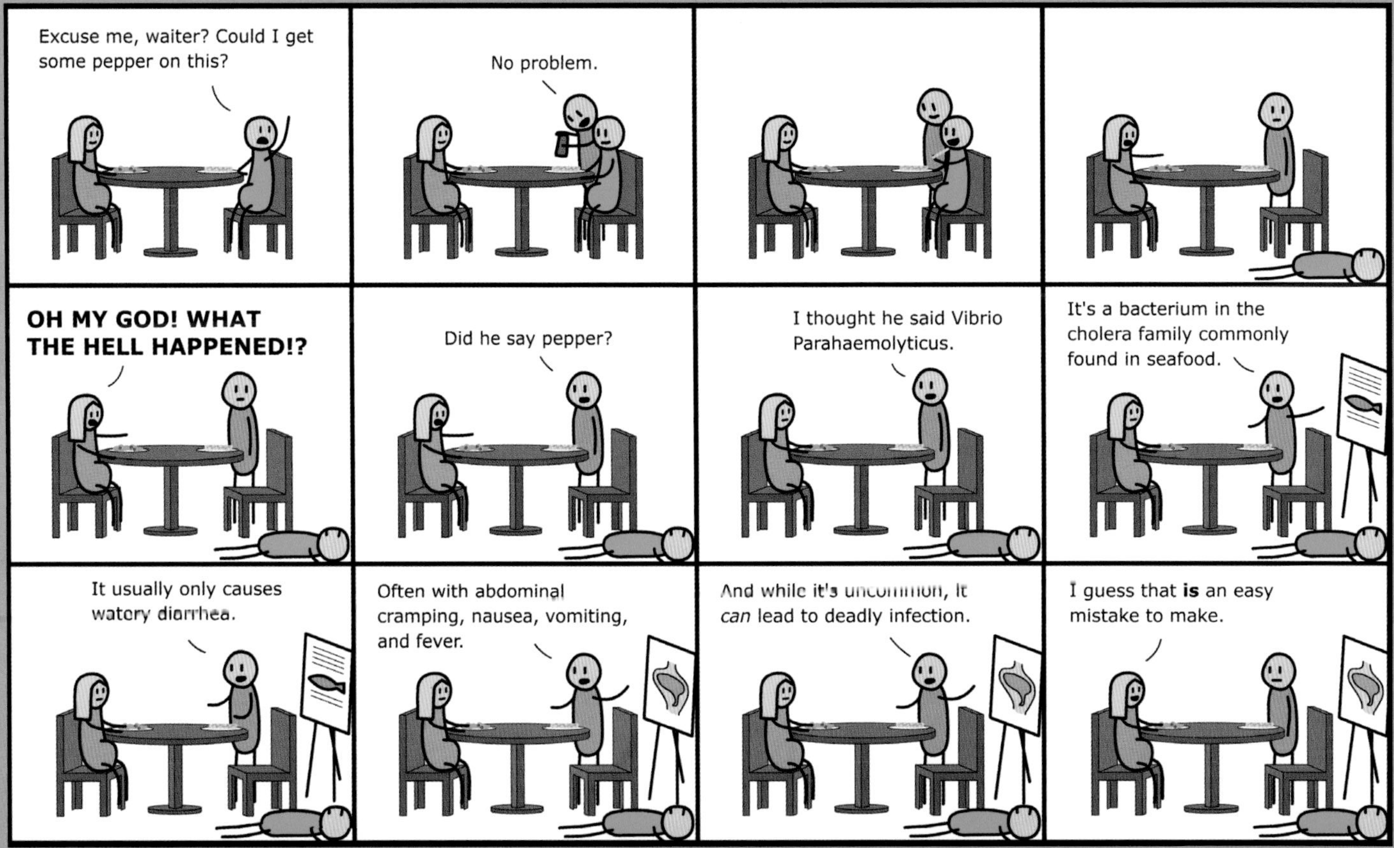
Excuse me, waiter? Could I get some pepper on this?
No problem.
OH MY GOD! WHAT THE HELL HAPPENED!?
Did he say pepper?
I thought he said Vibrio Parahaemolyticus.
It's a bacterium in the cholera family commonly found in seafood.
It usually only causes watery diarrhea.
Often with abdominal cramping, nausea, vomiting, and fever.
And while it's uncommon, it *can* lead to deadly infection.
I guess that **is** an easy mistake to make.

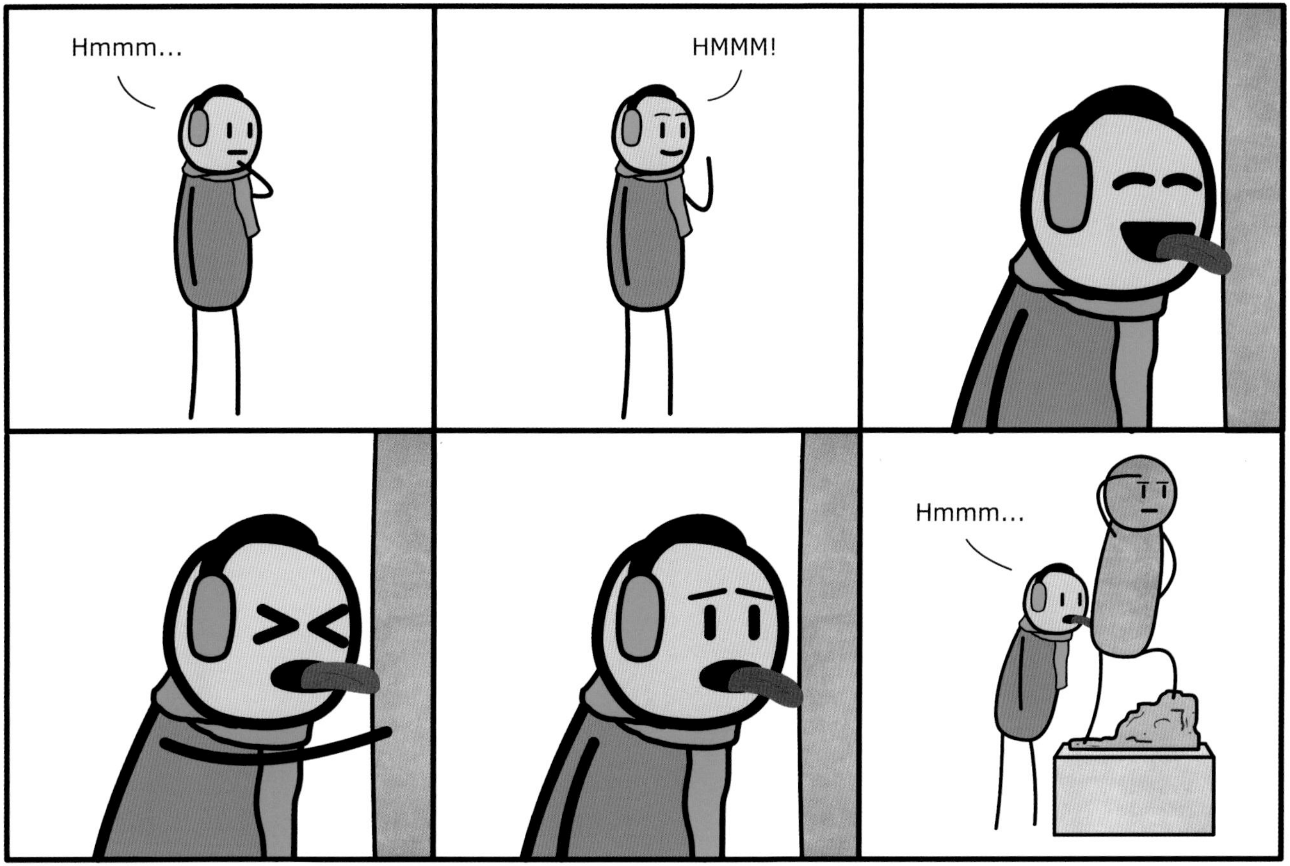
Hmmm...
HMMM!
Hmmm...

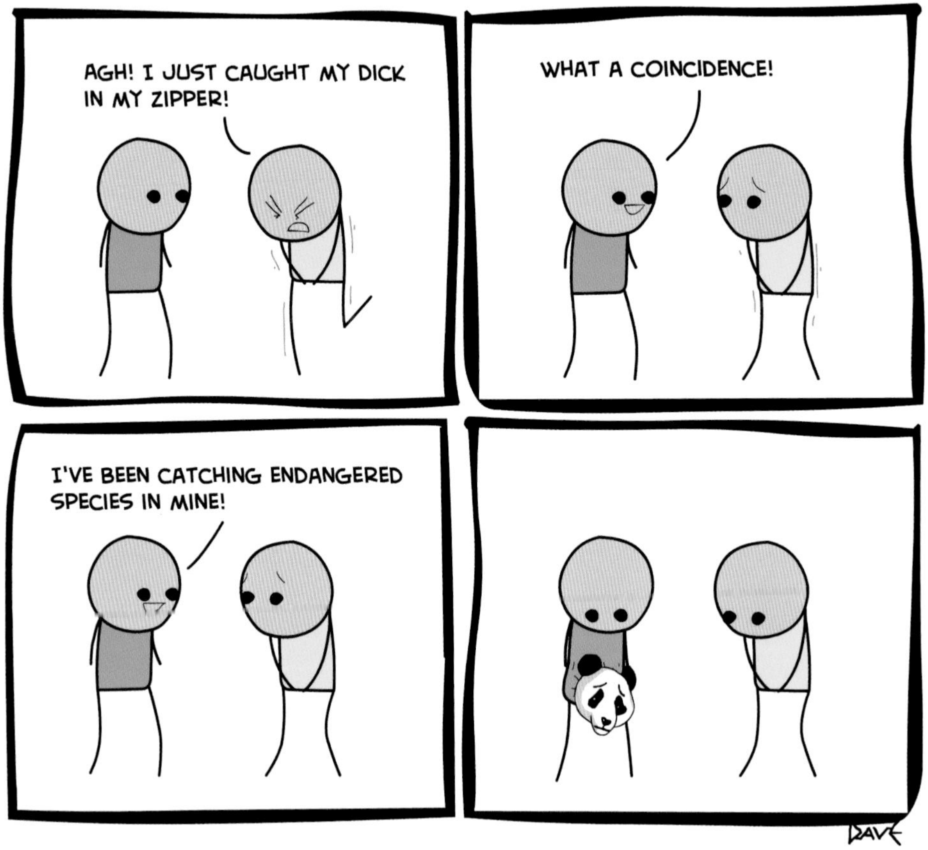
AGH! I JUST CAUGHT MY DICK IN MY ZIPPER!
WHAT A COINCIDENCE!
I'VE BEEN CATCHING ENDANGERED SPECIES IN MINE!
DAVE

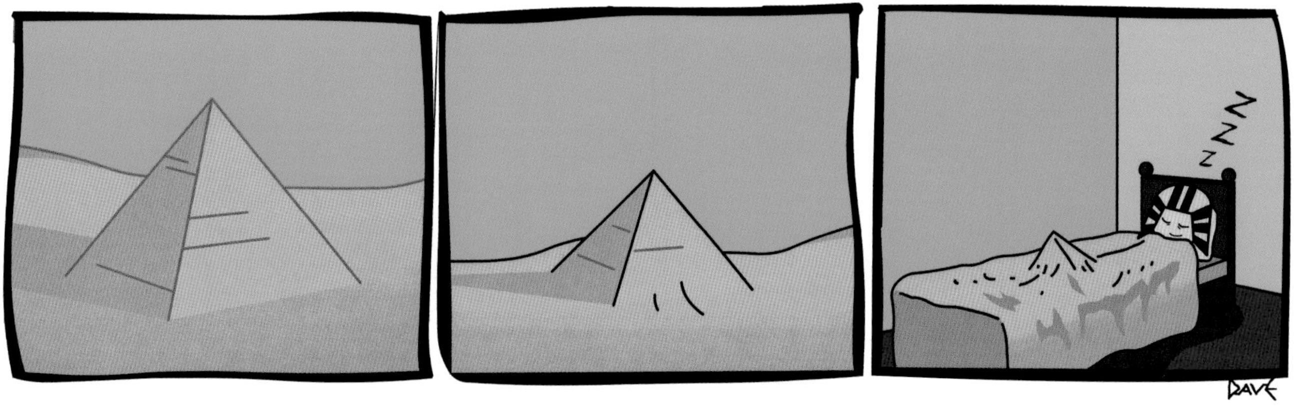
Z Z Z
DAVE

DADDY, HOW DO SQUIDS HAVE SEX?
WHY, THE SAME WAY I HAVE SEX!
WITH SQUIDS.

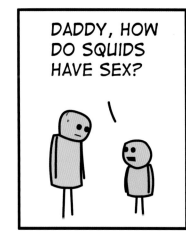

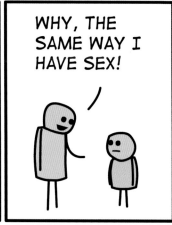

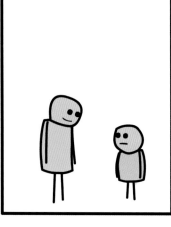

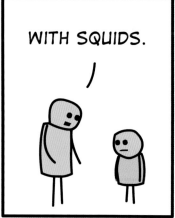

DID THE DOCTOR GIVE YOU YOUR TEST RESULTS?
YEAH. LOOKS LIKE ALL THOSE YEARS OF PHONE SEX CAUGHT UP WITH ME.
I HAVE HEARING AIDS.

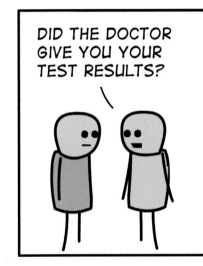

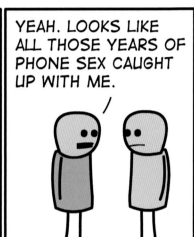

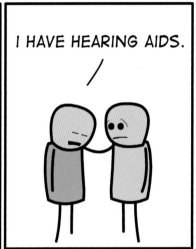

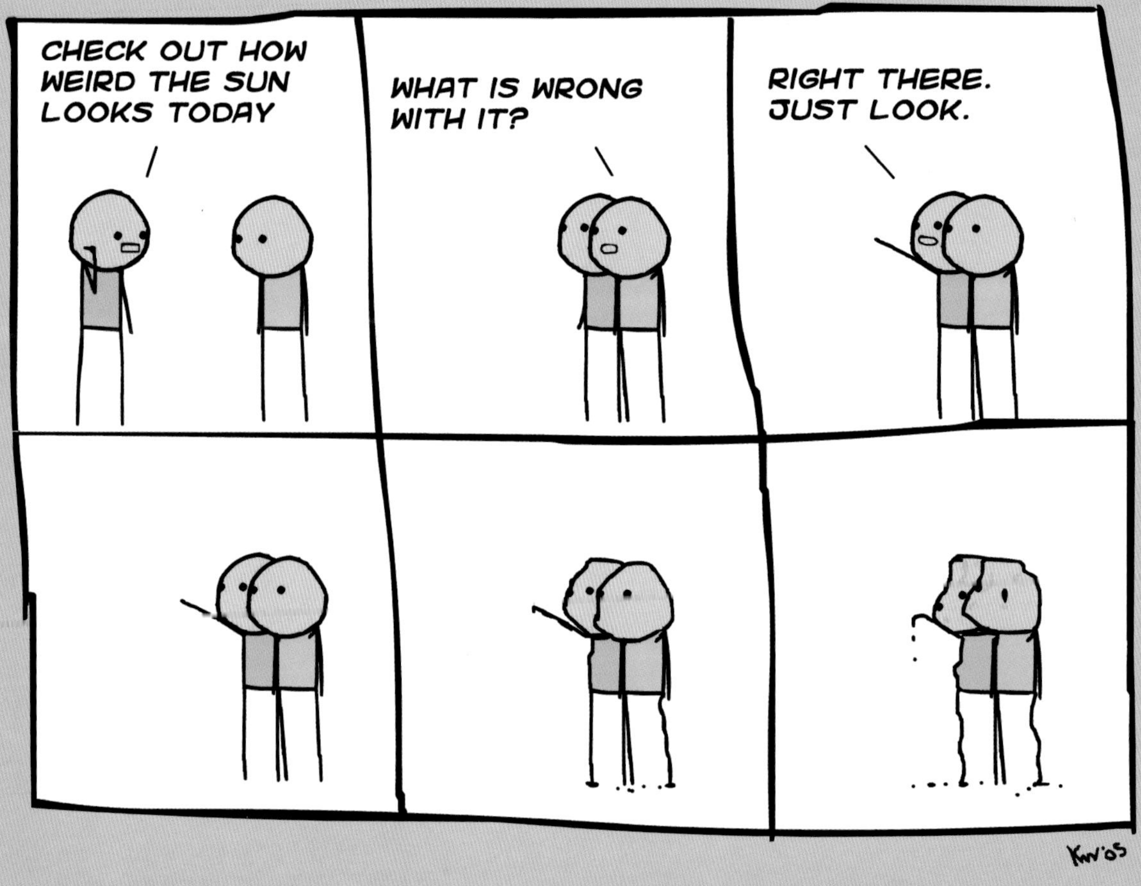
CHECK OUT HOW WEIRD THE SUN LOOKS TODAY
WHAT IS WRONG WITH IT?
RIGHT THERE. JUST LOOK.
Kw '05

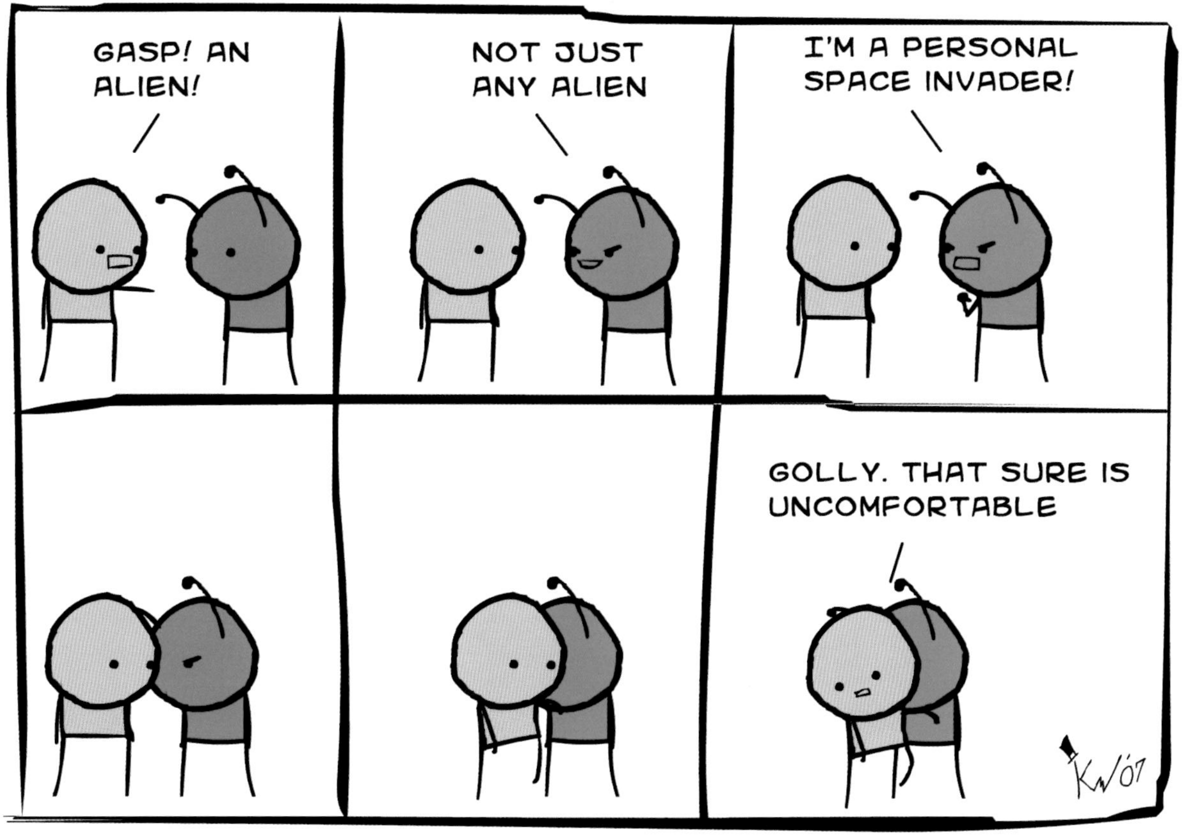
GASP! AN ALIEN!
NOT JUST ANY ALIEN
I'M A PERSONAL SPACE INVADER!
GOLLY. THAT SURE IS UNCOMFORTABLE
KW '07

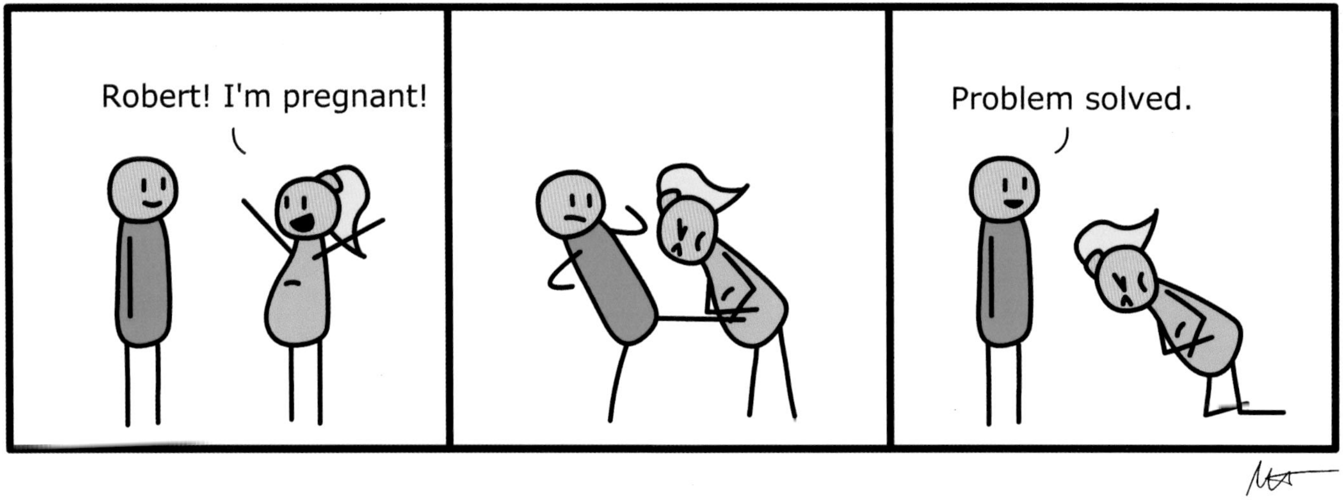
Robert! I'm pregnant!
Problem solved.

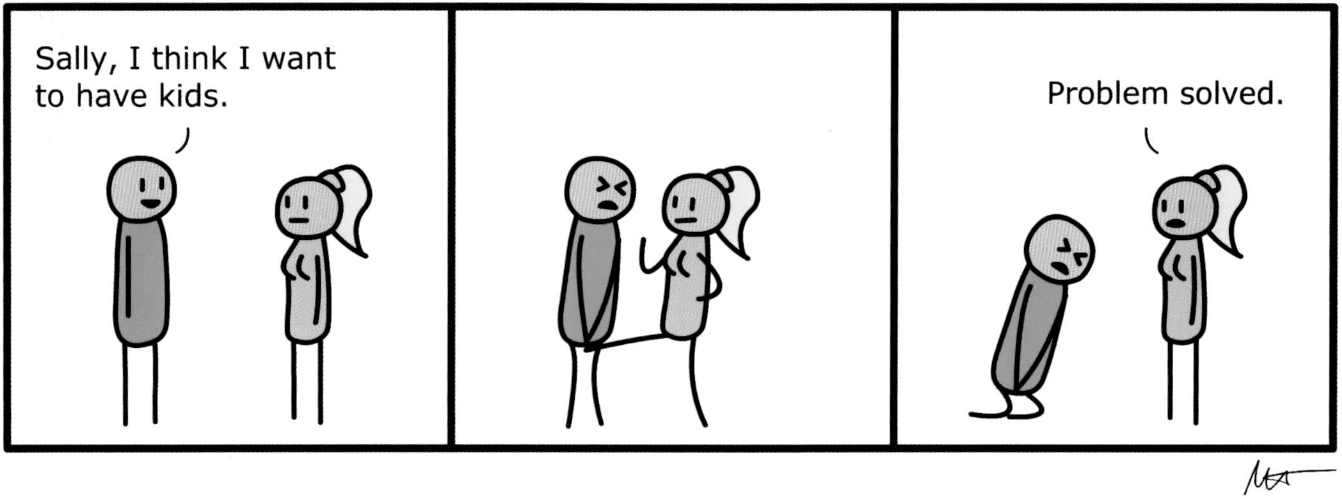
Sally, I think I want to have kids.
Problem solved.

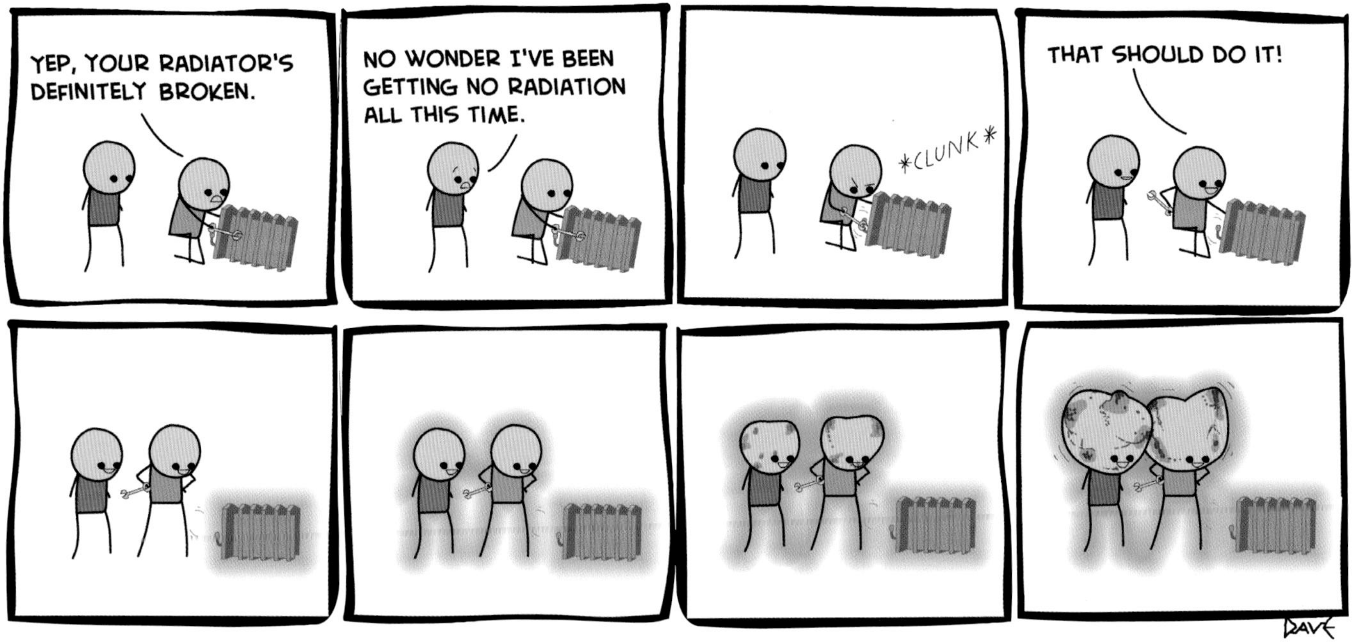
YEP, YOUR RADIATOR'S DEFINITELY BROKEN.
NO WONDER I'VE BEEN GETTING NO RADIATION ALL THIS TIME.
CLUNK
THAT SHOULD DO IT!
DAVE

AND AS YOU CAN SEE DOWN IN THE SOUTH WEST WE HAVE A LITTLE PRESSURE BUILDING UP...
WHILST UP NORTH YOU CAN EXPECT A FEW SCATTERED LIGHT SHOWERS.
MEANWHILE, OVER ON THE EAST COAST...
DAVE

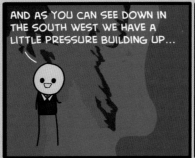

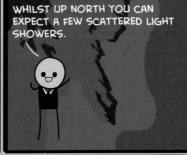

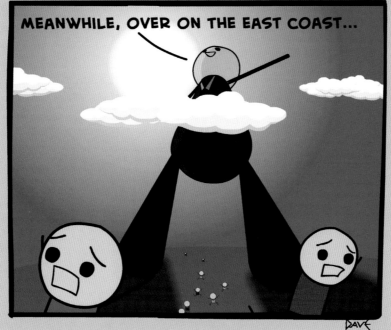

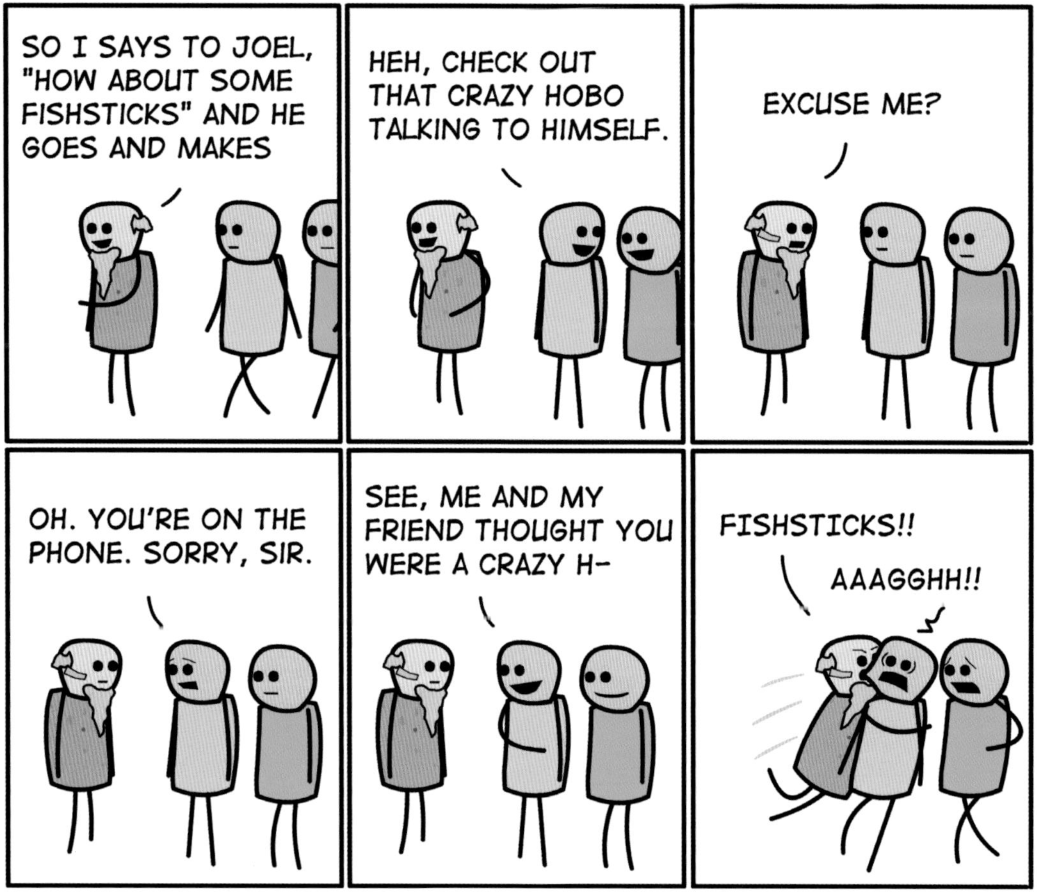
SO I SAYS TO JOEL, "HOW ABOUT SOME FISHSTICKS" AND HE GOES AND MAKES
HEH, CHECK OUT THAT CRAZY HOBO TALKING TO HIMSELF.
EXCUSE ME?
OH. YOU'RE ON THE PHONE. SORRY, SIR.
SEE, ME AND MY FRIEND THOUGHT YOU WERE A CRAZY H-
FISHSTICKS!!
AAAGGHH!!

YOU SHOULD SHAVE. THAT BEARD MAKES YOU LOOK LIKE AN AXE MURDERER.

IT'S ACTUALLY A MAGIC BEARD. IT VANISHES WHEN YOU'RE NOT LOOKING AT IT.

THAT'S SO COOL!! IS IT WORKING?!

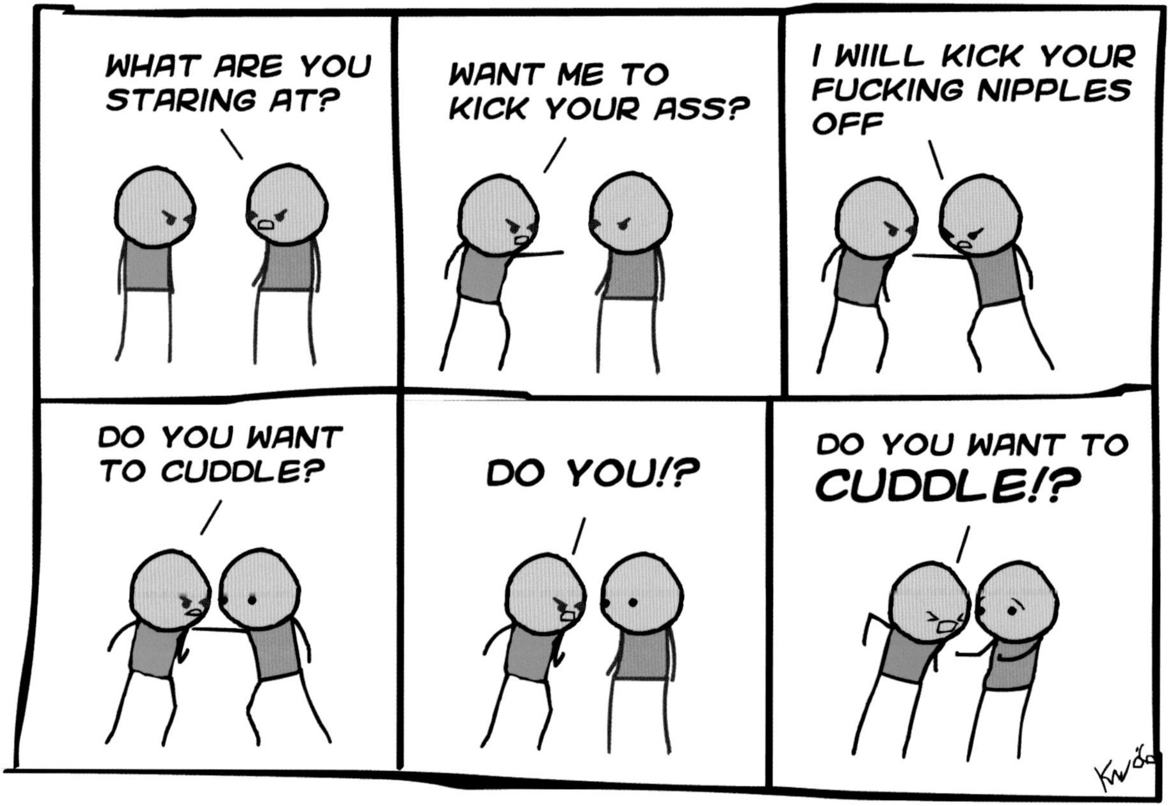
WHAT ARE YOU STARING AT?
WANT ME TO KICK YOUR ASS?
I WIILL KICK YOUR FUCKING NIPPLES OFF
DO YOU WANT TO CUDDLE?
DO YOU!?
DO YOU WANT TO CUDDLE!?

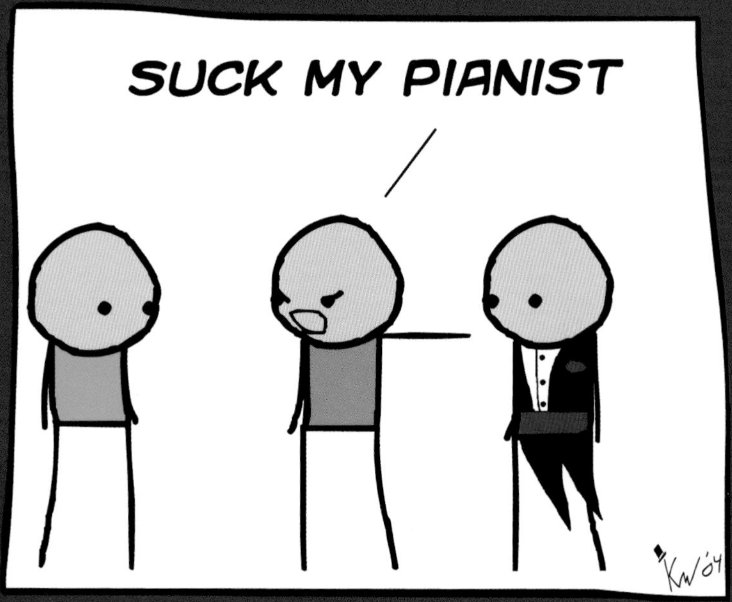
SUCK MY PIANIST
KW '04

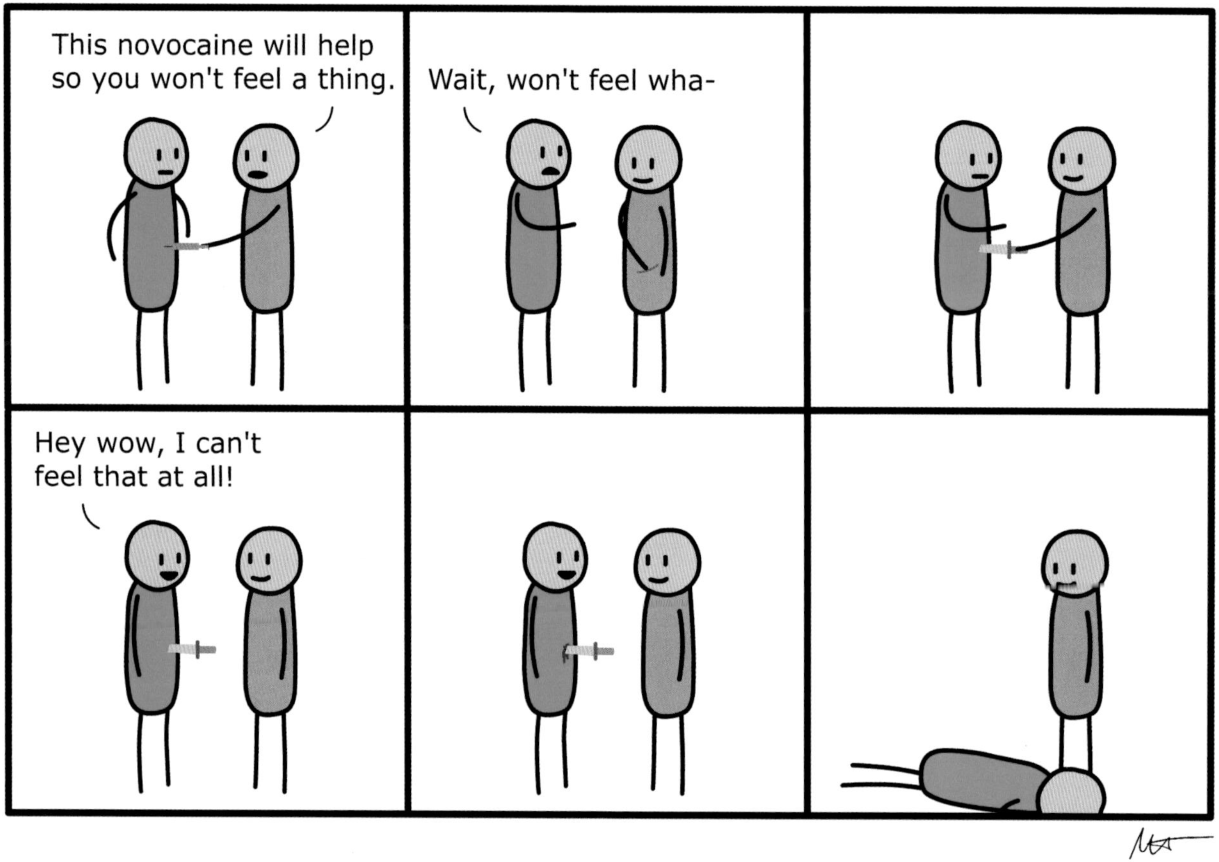
This novocaine will help so you won't feel a thing.
Wait, won't feel wha-
Hey wow, I can't feel that at all!

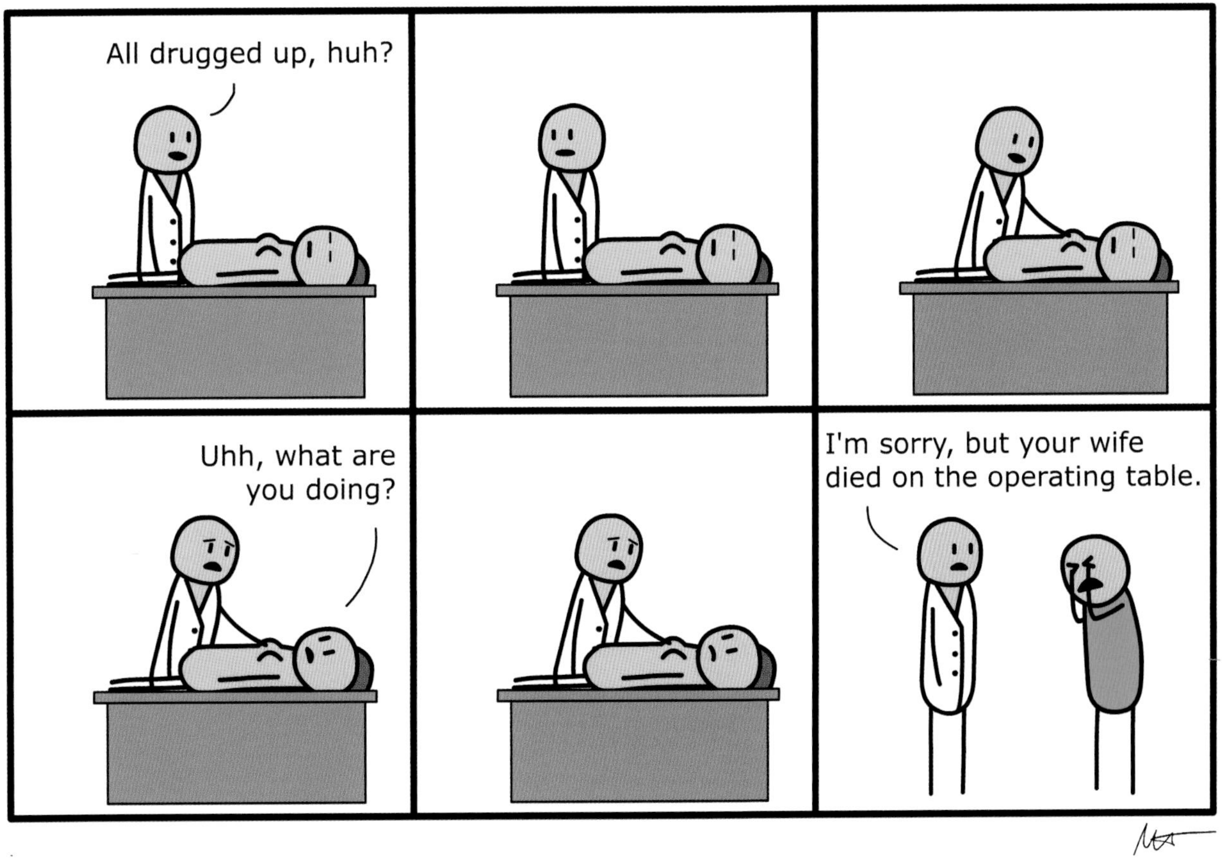
All drugged up, huh?
Uhh, what are you doing?
I'm sorry, but your wife died on the operating table.

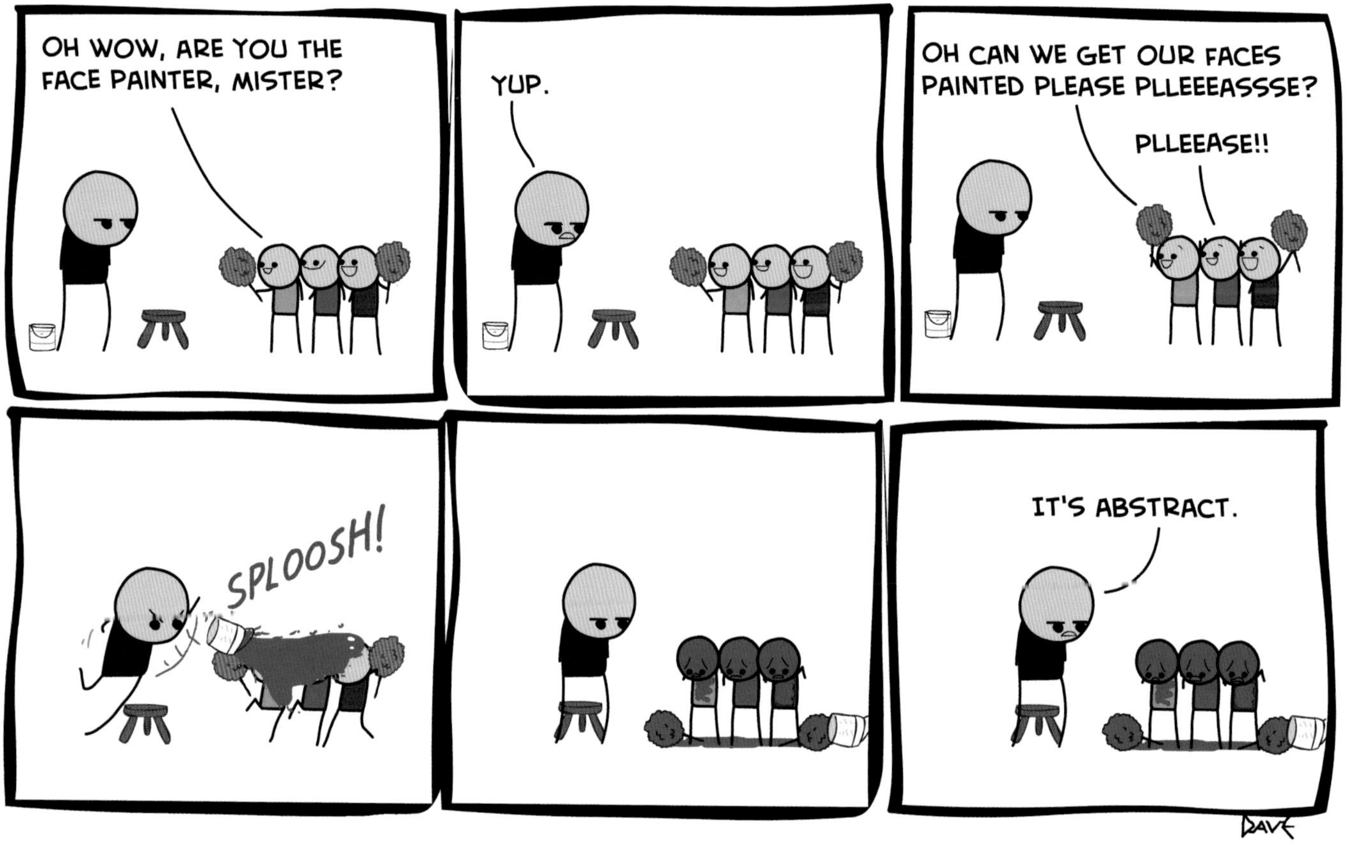
OH WOW, ARE YOU THE FACE PAINTER, MISTER?
YUP.
OH CAN WE GET OUR FACES PAINTED PLEASE PLLEEEASSSE?
PLLEEASE!!
SPLOOSH!
IT'S ABSTRACT.
DAVE

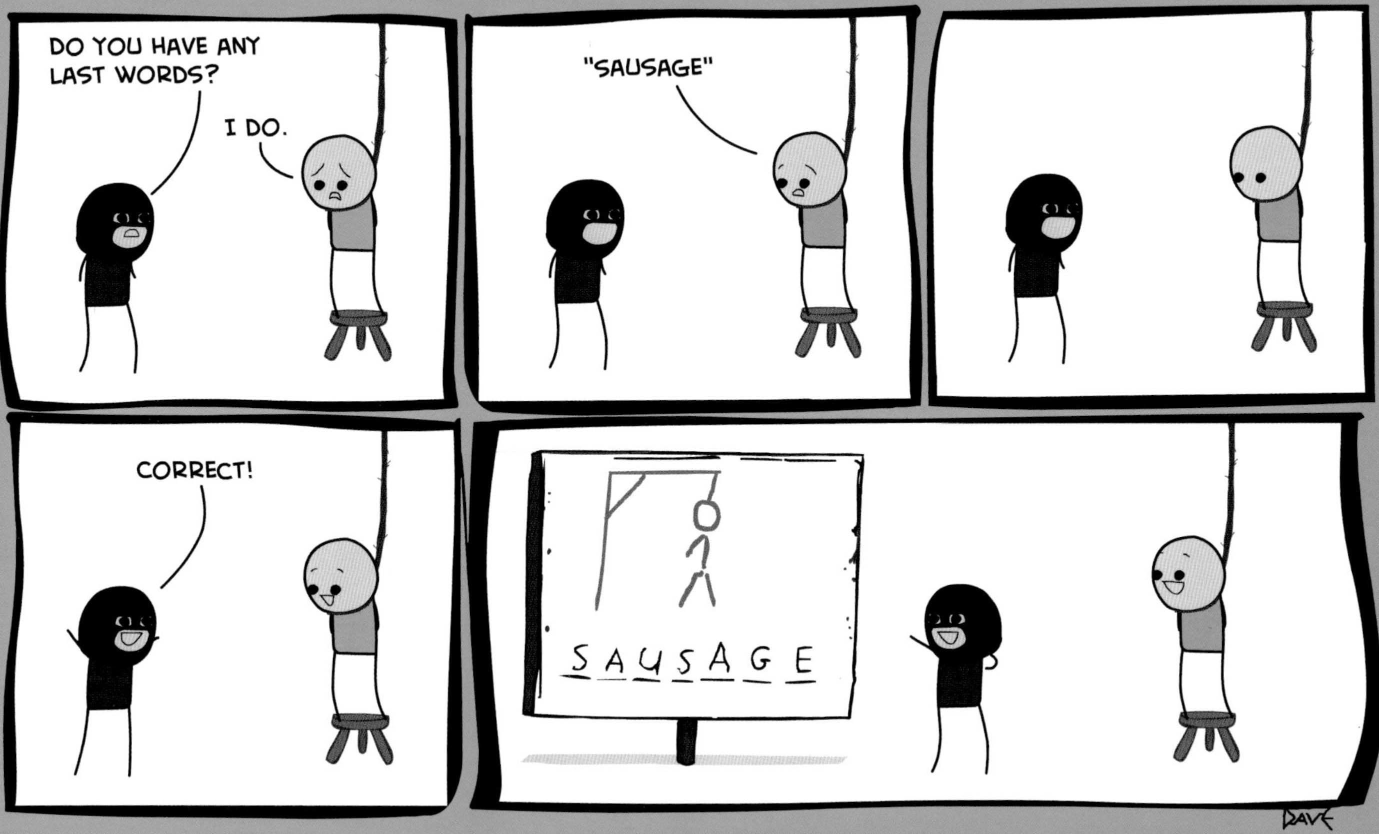
DO YOU HAVE ANY LAST WORDS?
I DO.
"SAUSAGE"
CORRECT!
SAUSAGE
DAVE

WOULD YOU HAVE SEX WITH TWELVE DUDES AT ONCE FOR A MILLION DOLLARS?
DEFINITELY.
I'D PAY *ANYTHING* TO HAVE SEX WITH TWELVE DUDES AT ONCE.

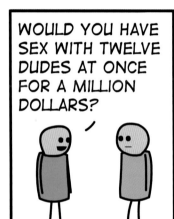

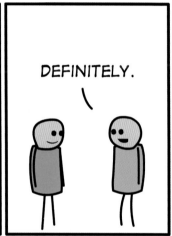

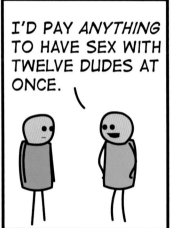

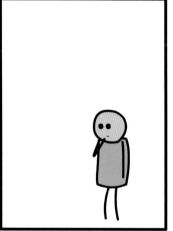

WHAT'S IN THE BRIEFCASE?
A SMALLER BRIEFCASE. AND THEN A SMALLER ONE INSIDE THAT ONE.
HA HA! WHAT'S INSIDE THE SMALLEST ONE?
CHILD PORN.

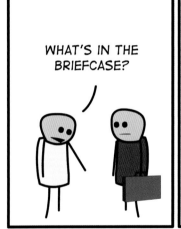

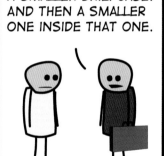

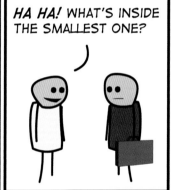

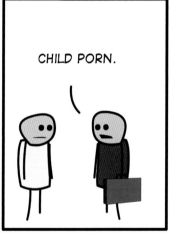

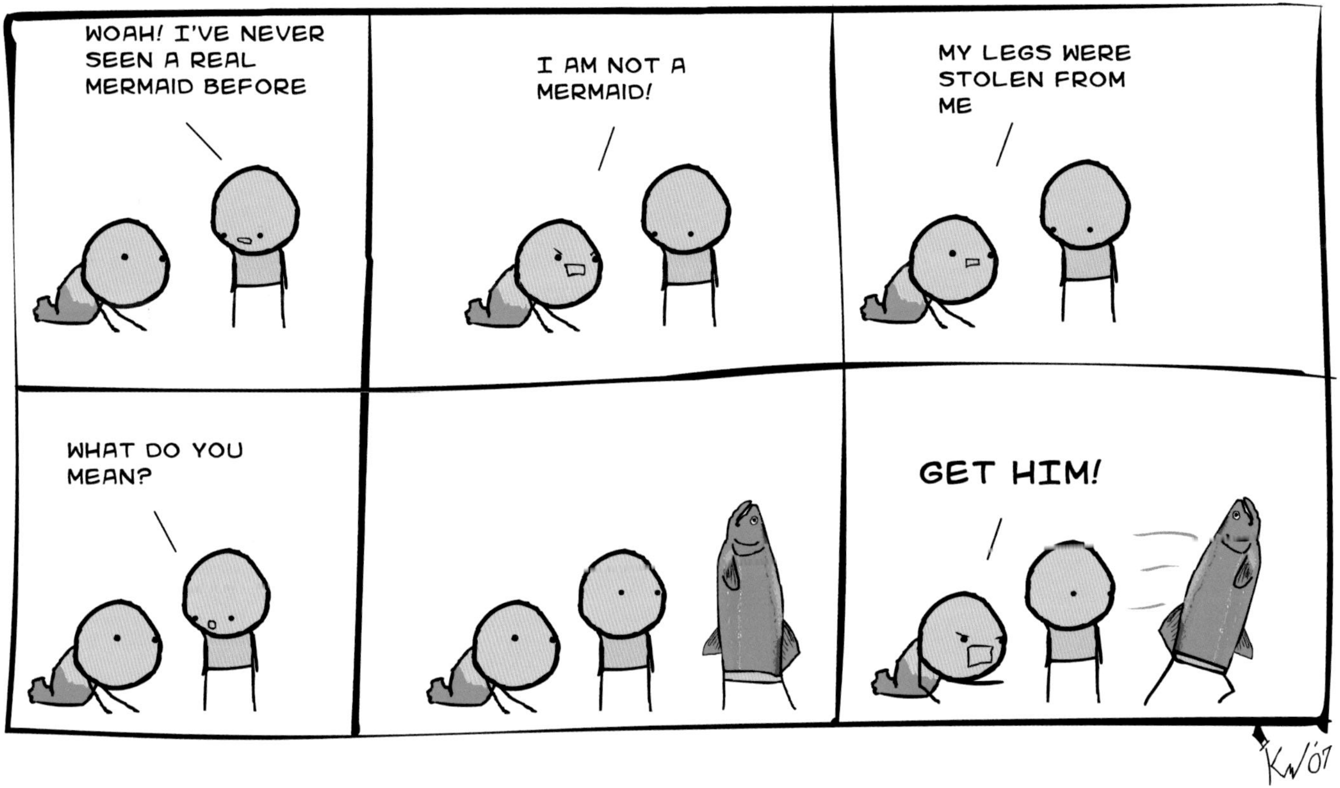
WOAH! I'VE NEVER SEEN A REAL MERMAID BEFORE
I AM NOT A MERMAID!
MY LEGS WERE STOLEN FROM ME
WHAT DO YOU MEAN?
GET HIM!
KW '07

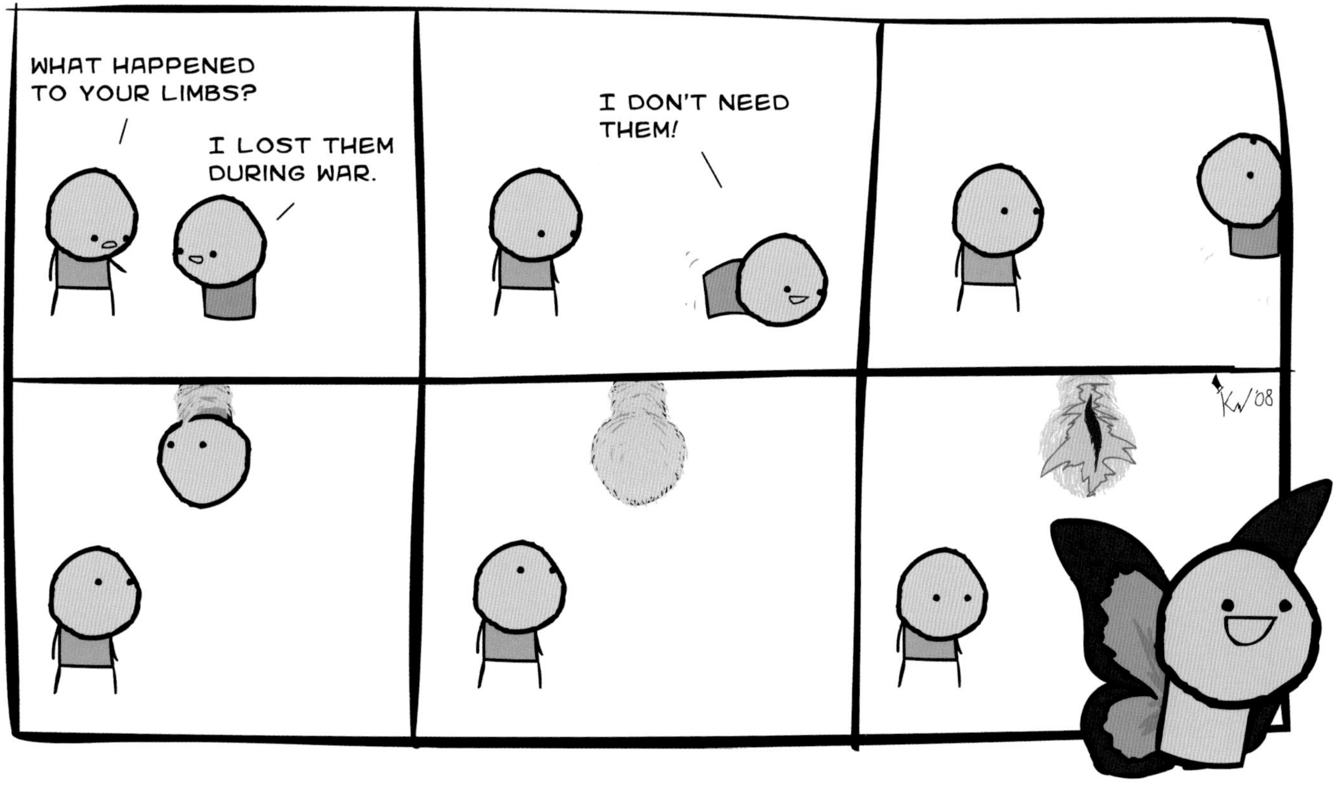
WHAT HAPPENED TO YOUR LIMBS?
I LOST THEM DURING WAR.
I DON'T NEED THEM!
KW '08

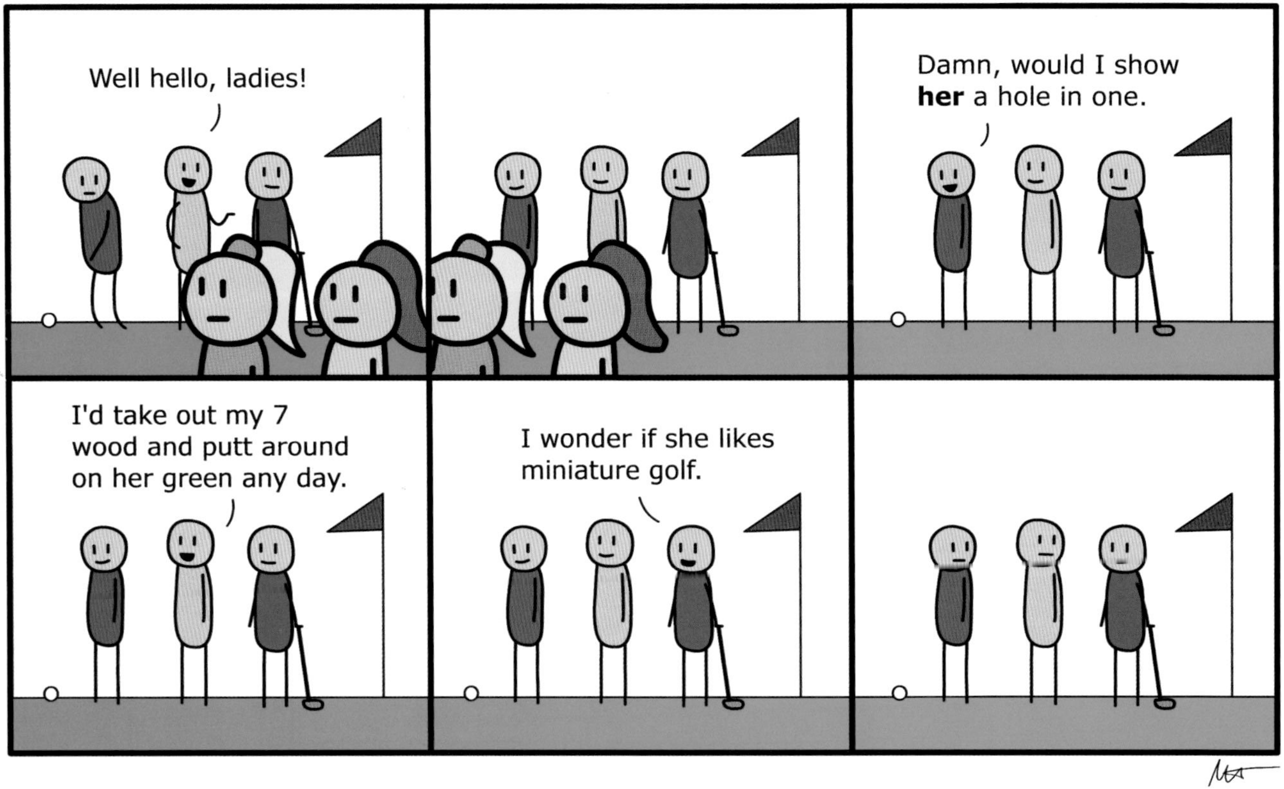
Well hello, ladies!
Damn, would I show **her** a hole in one.
I'd take out my 7 wood and putt around on her green any day.
I wonder if she likes miniature golf.

Why, hello there.
Oh! Hi...
Is this seat taken?
Not at all.
Cool! Thanks!

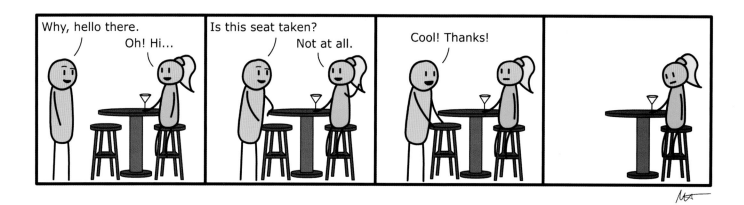

OW! OH!
ARGH!
DAVE

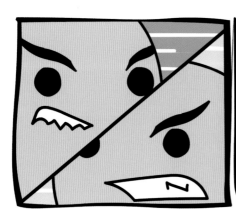

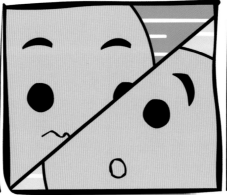

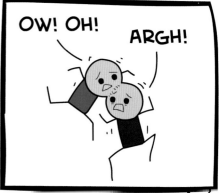

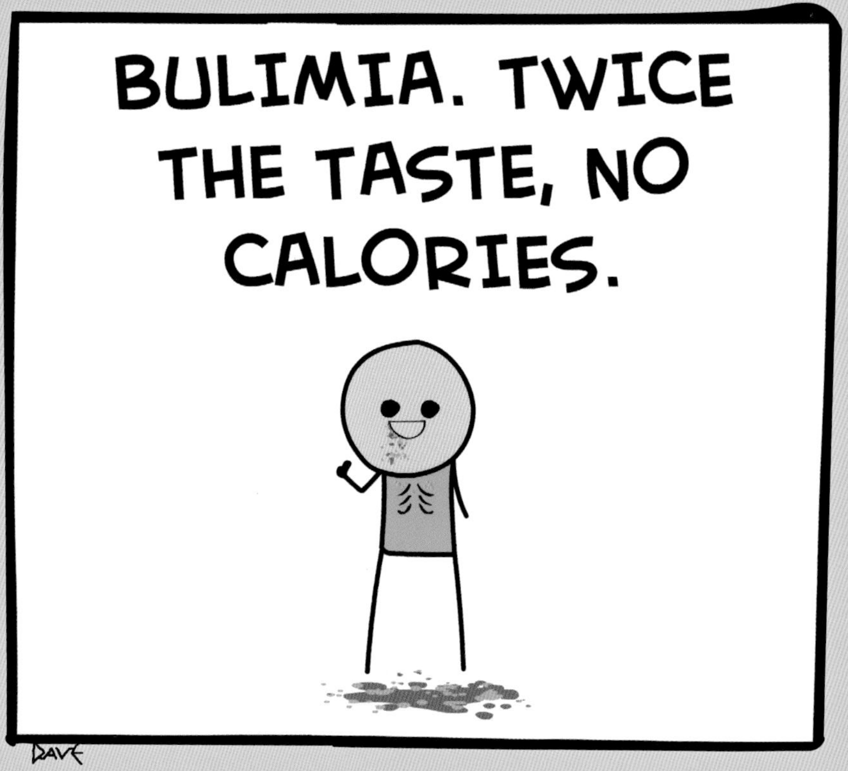
BULIMIA. TWICE THE TASTE, NO CALORIES.
DAVE

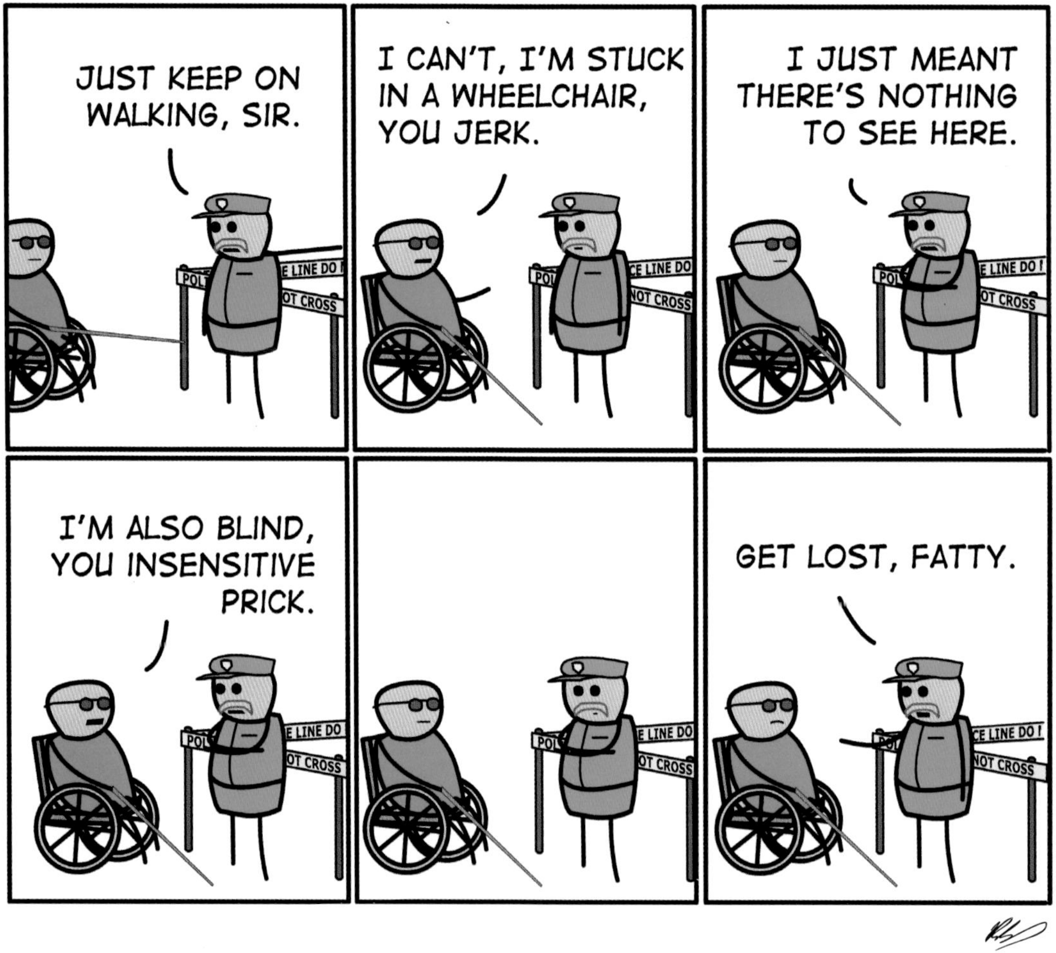
JUST KEEP ON WALKING, SIR.
I CAN'T, I'M STUCK IN A WHEELCHAIR, YOU JERK.
I JUST MEANT THERE'S NOTHING TO SEE HERE.
I'M ALSO BLIND, YOU INSENSITIVE PRICK.
GET LOST, FATTY.

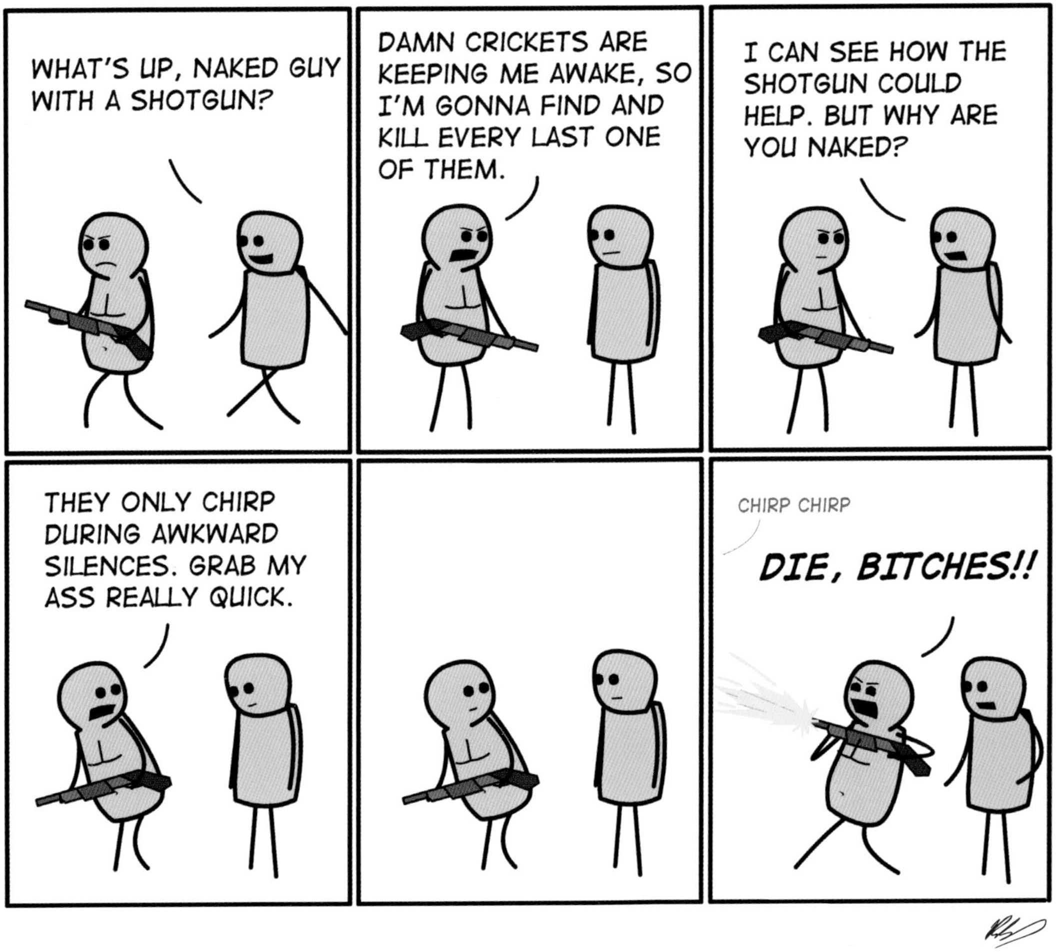
WHAT'S UP, NAKED GUY WITH A SHOTGUN?
DAMN CRICKETS ARE KEEPING ME AWAKE, SO I'M GONNA FIND AND KILL EVERY LAST ONE OF THEM.
I CAN SEE HOW THE SHOTGUN COULD HELP. BUT WHY ARE YOU NAKED?
THEY ONLY CHIRP DURING AWKWARD SILENCES. GRAB MY ASS REALLY QUICK.
CHIRP CHIRP
DIE, BITCHES!!

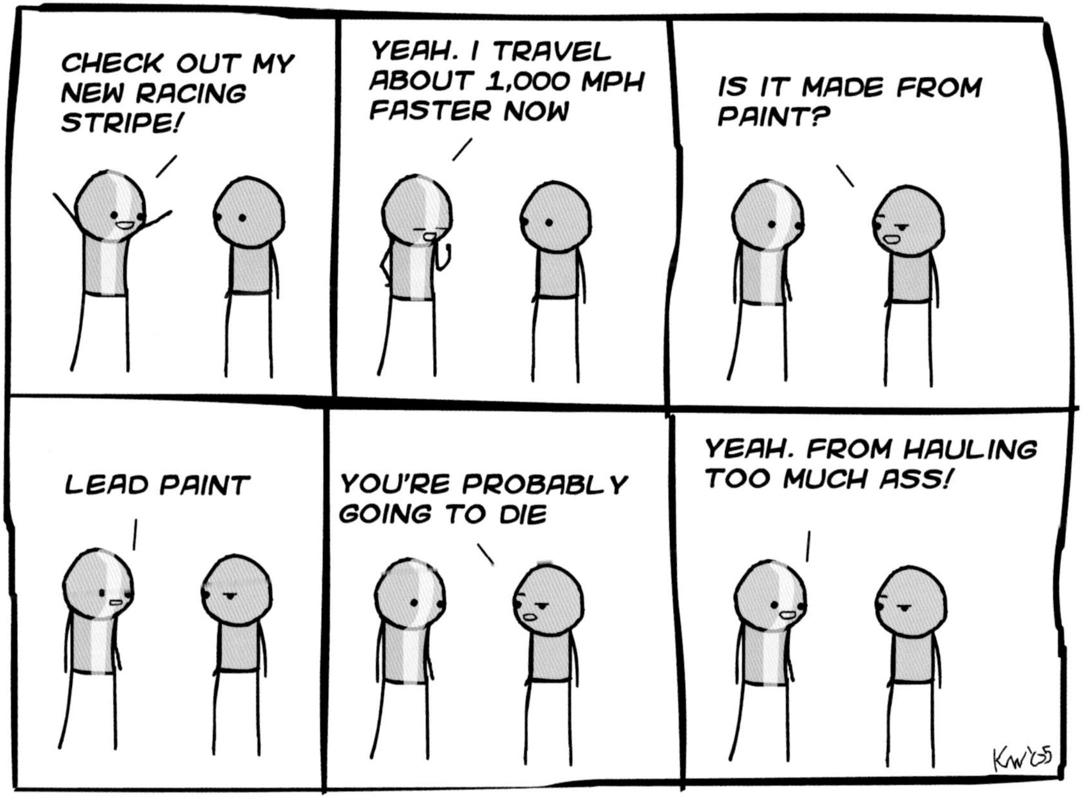
CHECK OUT MY NEW RACING STRIPE!
YEAH. I TRAVEL ABOUT 1,000 MPH FASTER NOW
IS IT MADE FROM PAINT?
LEAD PAINT
YOU'RE PROBABLY GOING TO DIE
YEAH. FROM HAULING TOO MUCH ASS!

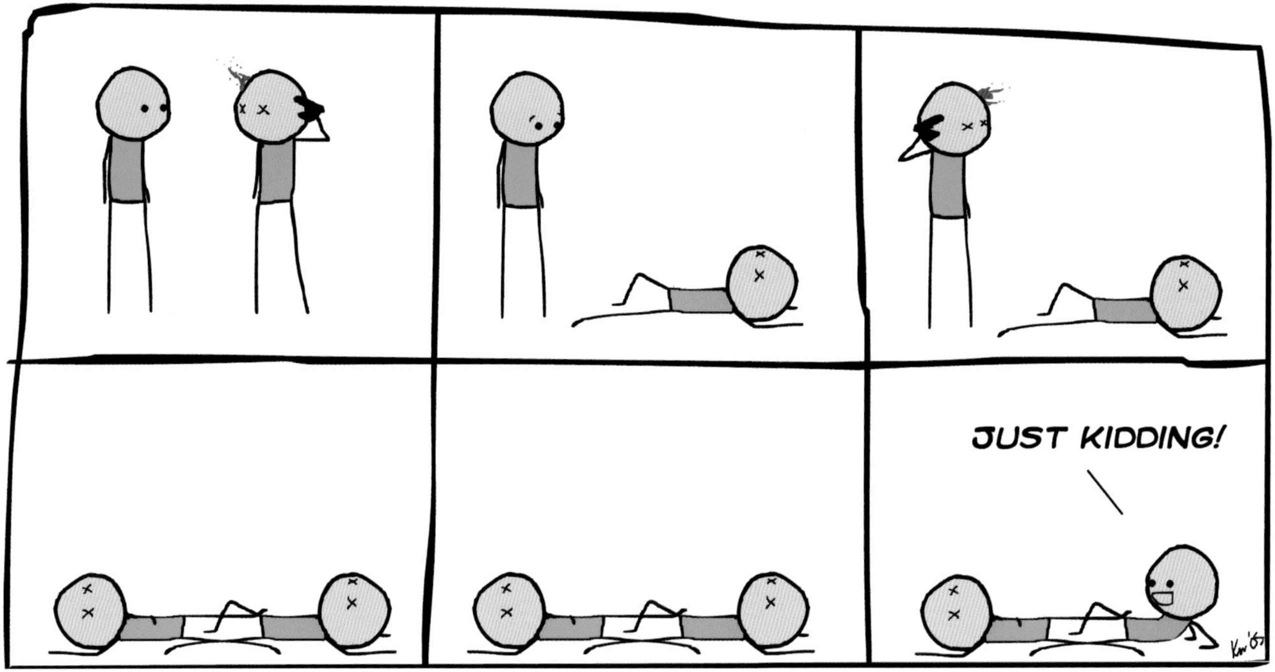
JUST KIDDING!
Kris '05

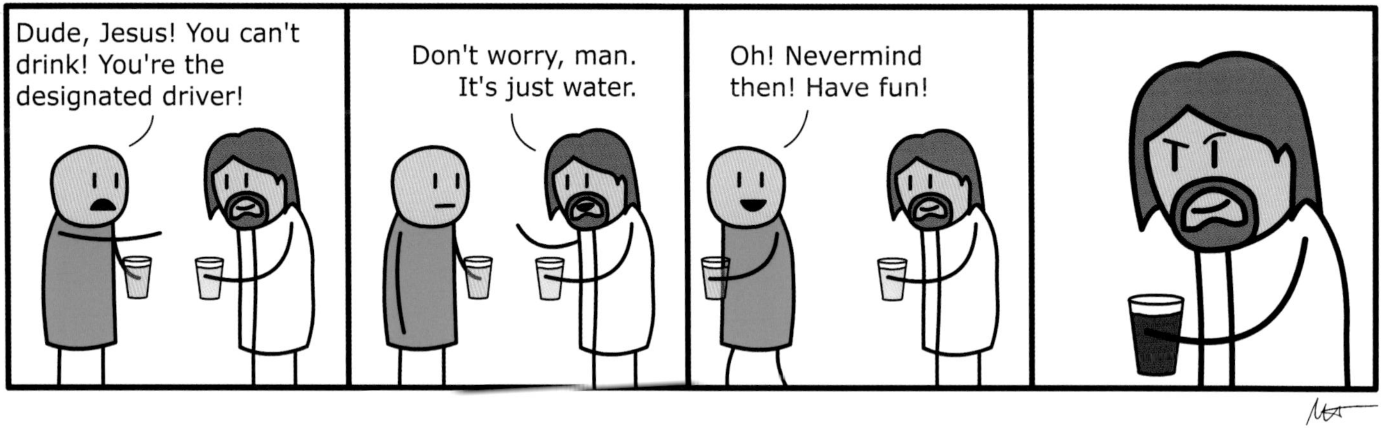
Dude, Jesus! You can't drink! You're the designated driver!
Don't worry, man. It's just water.
Oh! Nevermind then! Have fun!

The Pros and Cons of Being Post-Crucifixion Jesus Christ

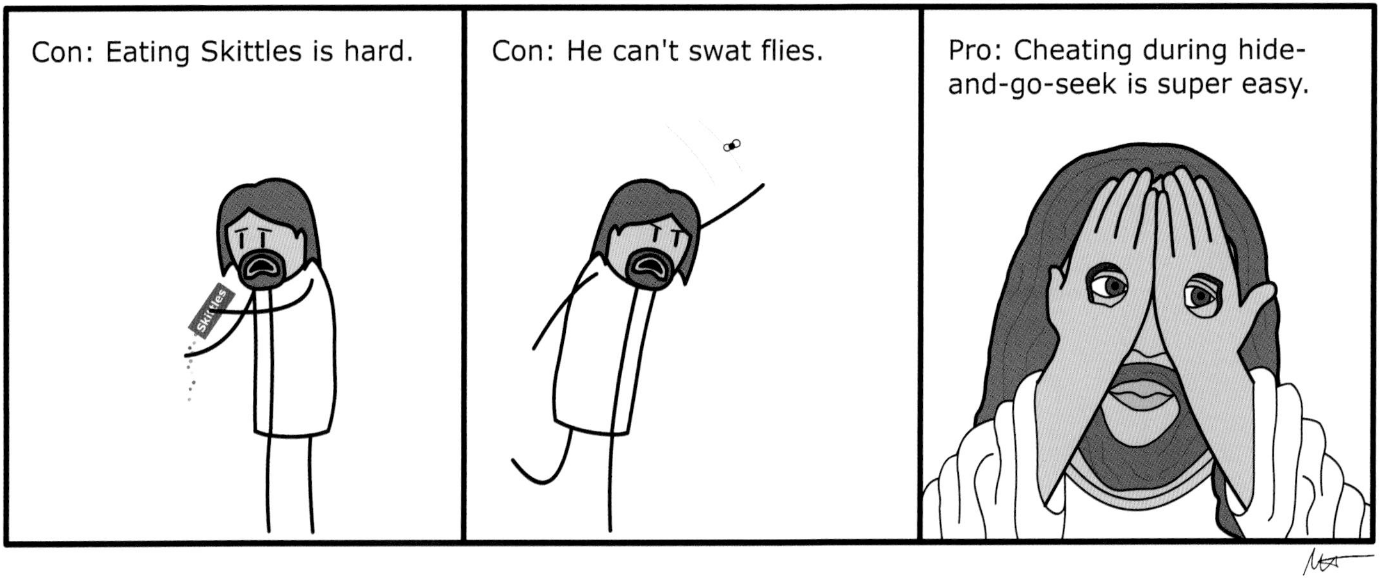
Con: Eating Skittles is hard.
Skittles
Con: He can't swat flies.
Pro: Cheating during hide-and-go-seek is super easy.

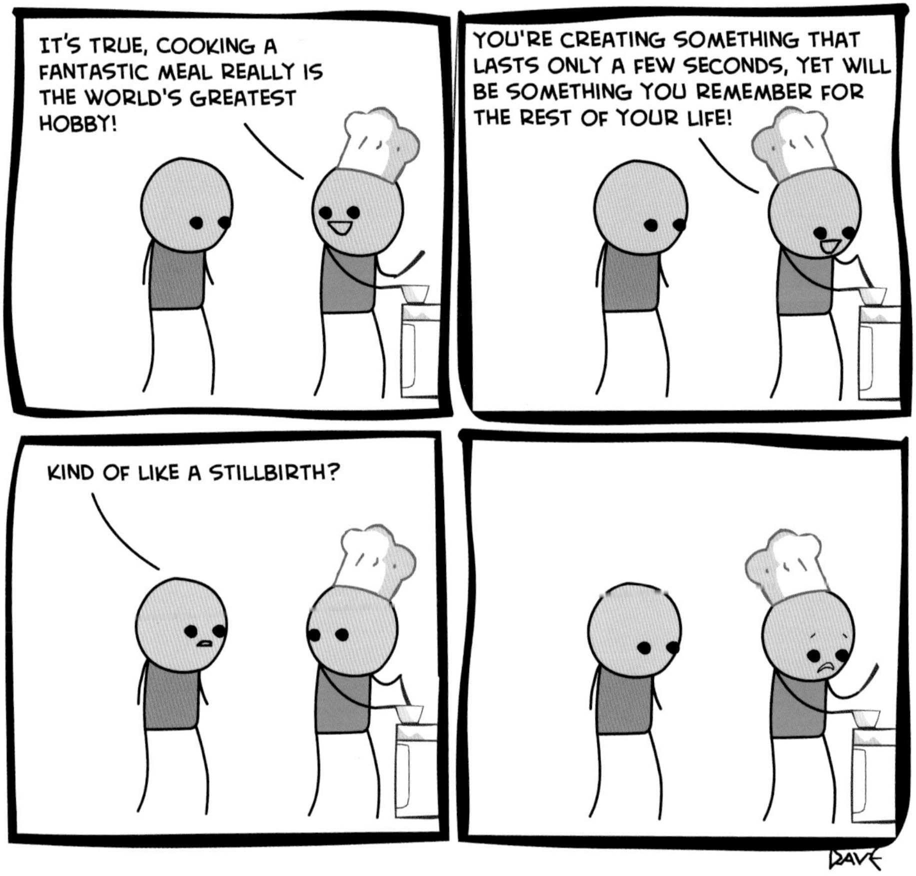
IT'S TRUE, COOKING A FANTASTIC MEAL REALLY IS THE WORLD'S GREATEST HOBBY!
YOU'RE CREATING SOMETHING THAT LASTS ONLY A FEW SECONDS, YET WILL BE SOMETHING YOU REMEMBER FOR THE REST OF YOUR LIFE!
KIND OF LIKE A STILLBIRTH?
DAVE

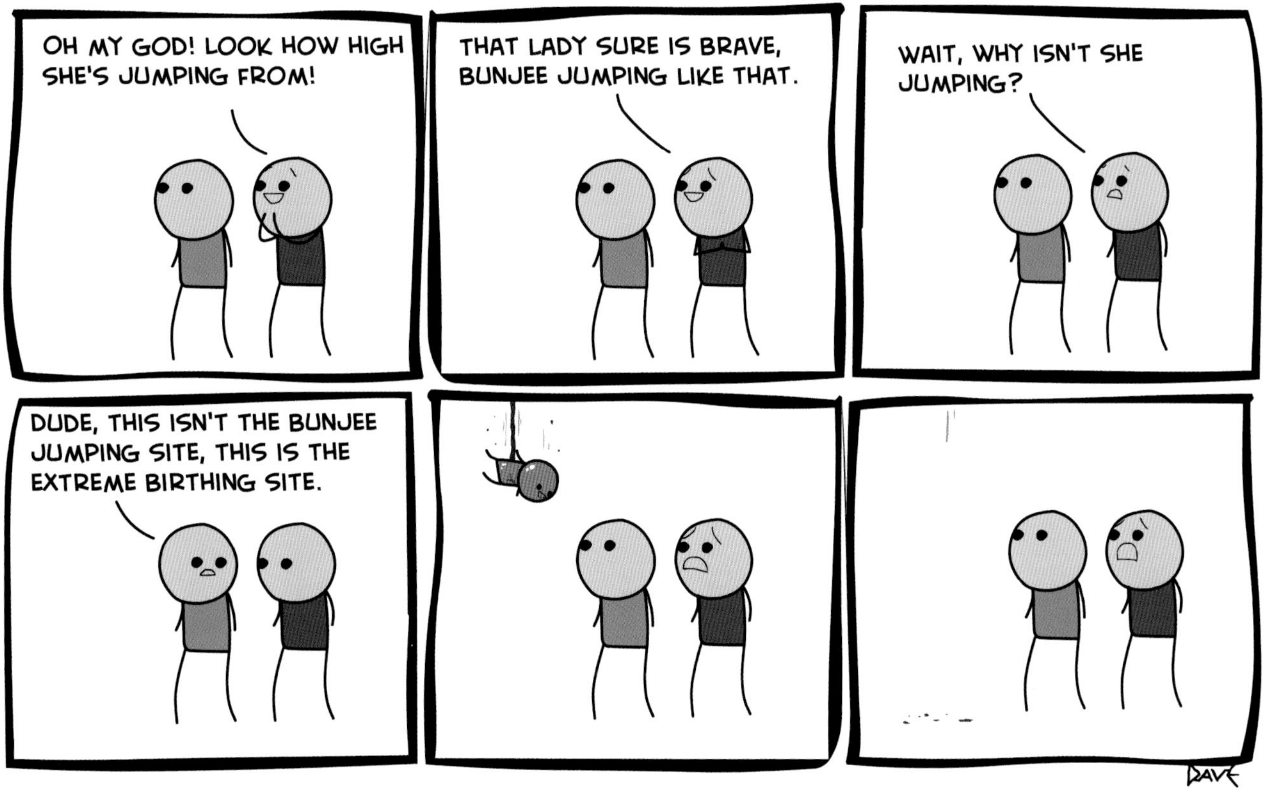

OH MY GOD! LOOK HOW HIGH SHE'S JUMPING FROM!
THAT LADY SURE IS BRAVE, BUNJEE JUMPING LIKE THAT.
WAIT, WHY ISN'T SHE JUMPING?
DUDE, THIS ISN'T THE BUNJEE JUMPING SITE, THIS IS THE EXTREME BIRTHING SITE.
DAVE

HEY BABY, CAN I TAKE YOUR CLOTHES OFF WITH MY TEETH?
YOU CAN DO ANYTHING YOU WANT.
MMM...
...MMFF YEAH...
...THOTHE ARE THUM FUGGIN GOOD CLOTHTH.

BABY, I JUST REALIZED I CAN'T SURVIVE WITHOUT YOU.
IS IT BECAUSE YOU LOVE ME?
IT'S BECAUSE YOU'RE AN ORGAN DONOR.

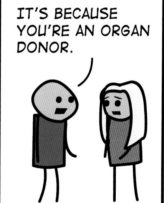

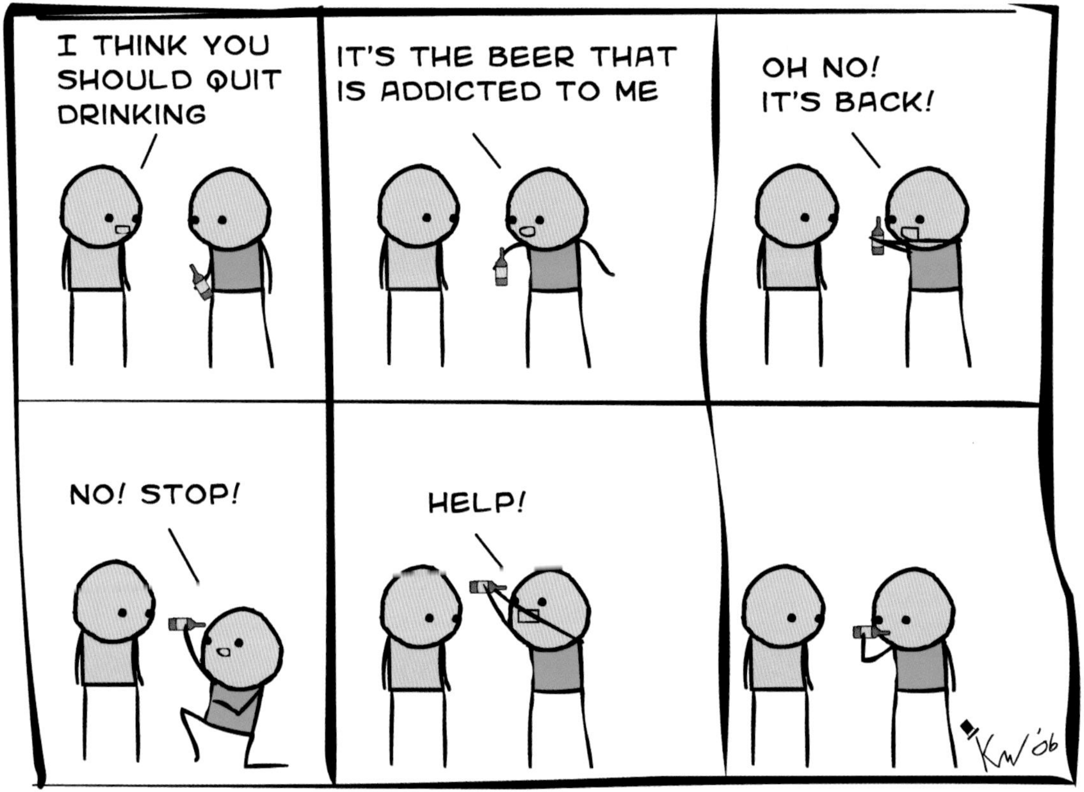

I THINK YOU SHOULD QUIT DRINKING
IT'S THE BEER THAT IS ADDICTED TO ME
OH NO! IT'S BACK!
NO! STOP!
HELP!
KW '06

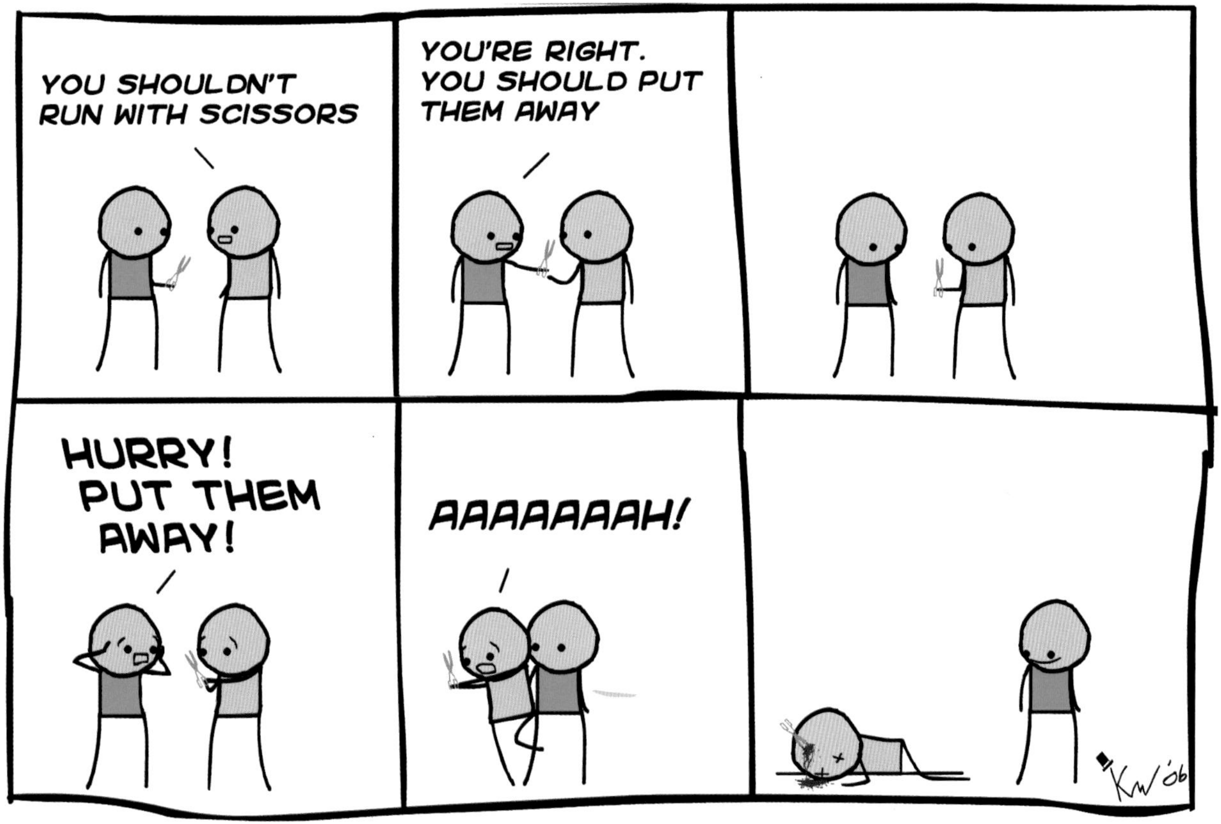
YOU SHOULDN'T RUN WITH SCISSORS
YOU'RE RIGHT. YOU SHOULD PUT THEM AWAY
HURRY! PUT THEM AWAY!
AAAAAAAH!
KW '06

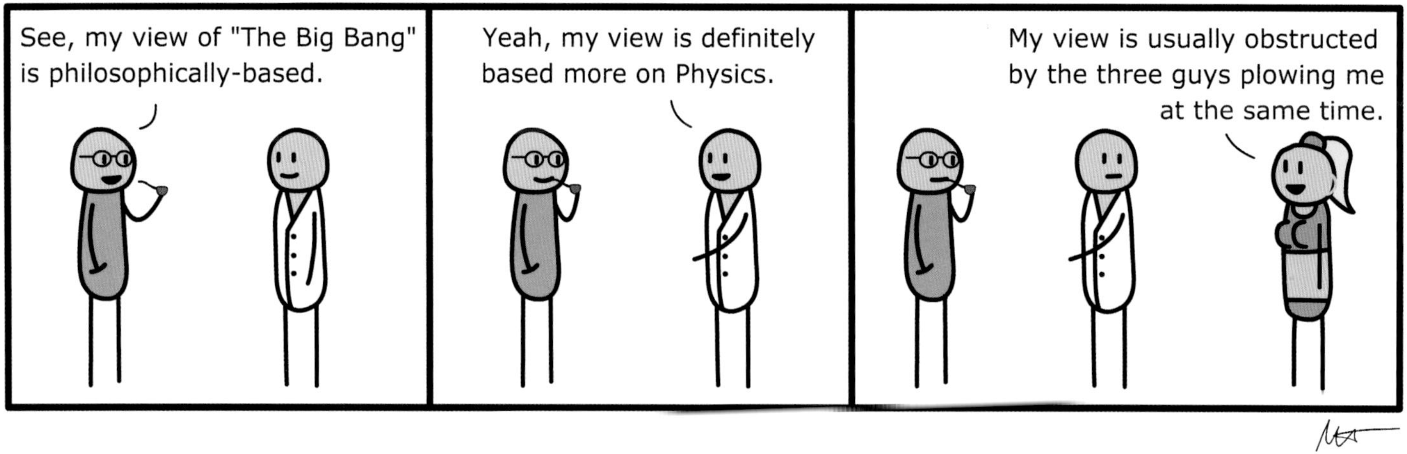
See, my view of "The Big Bang" is philosophically-based.
Yeah, my view is definitely based more on Physics.
My view is usually obstructed by the three guys plowing me at the same time.

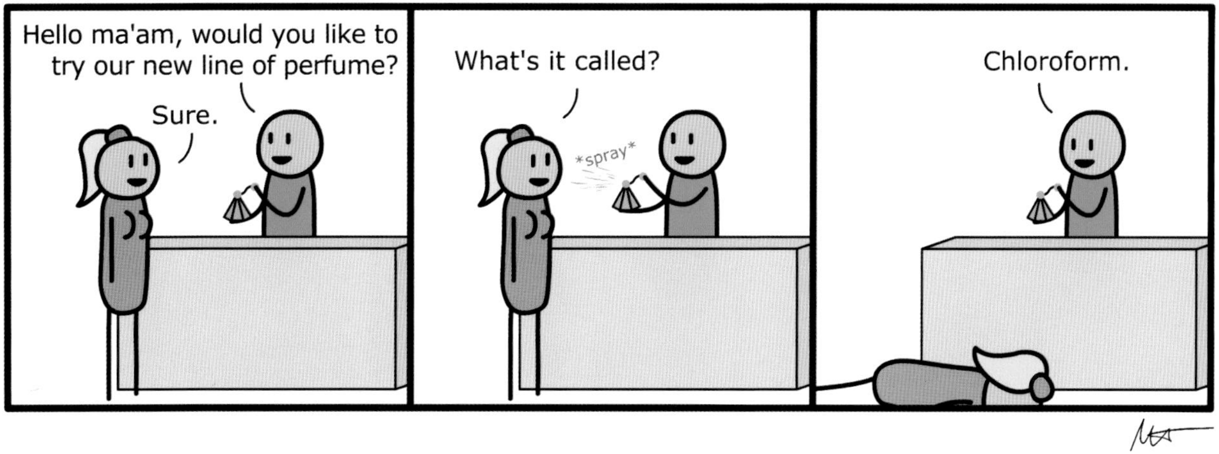
Hello ma'am, would you like to try our new line of perfume?
Sure.
What's it called?
spray
Chloroform.

I'LL BE BACK.
NO WAY DUDE, I WANNA BE BACK!
DAVE

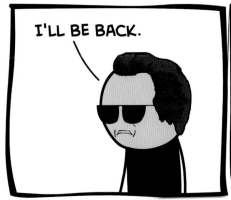

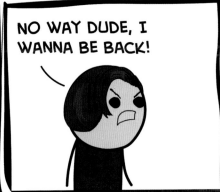

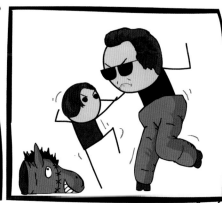

HEY DUDE, EVER SEEN A SNAKE SMILE?
NO.
ZIP
OH MY GOD!!!
GREAT, NOW JUST HOLD THAT POSE.
DAVE

OH GOD, MY HOUSE IS ON FIRE!!!
WAIT... ARE THESE... ARE THESE DECALS?
YO HOUSE JUST GOT PIMPED!!
OH MY GOD!!

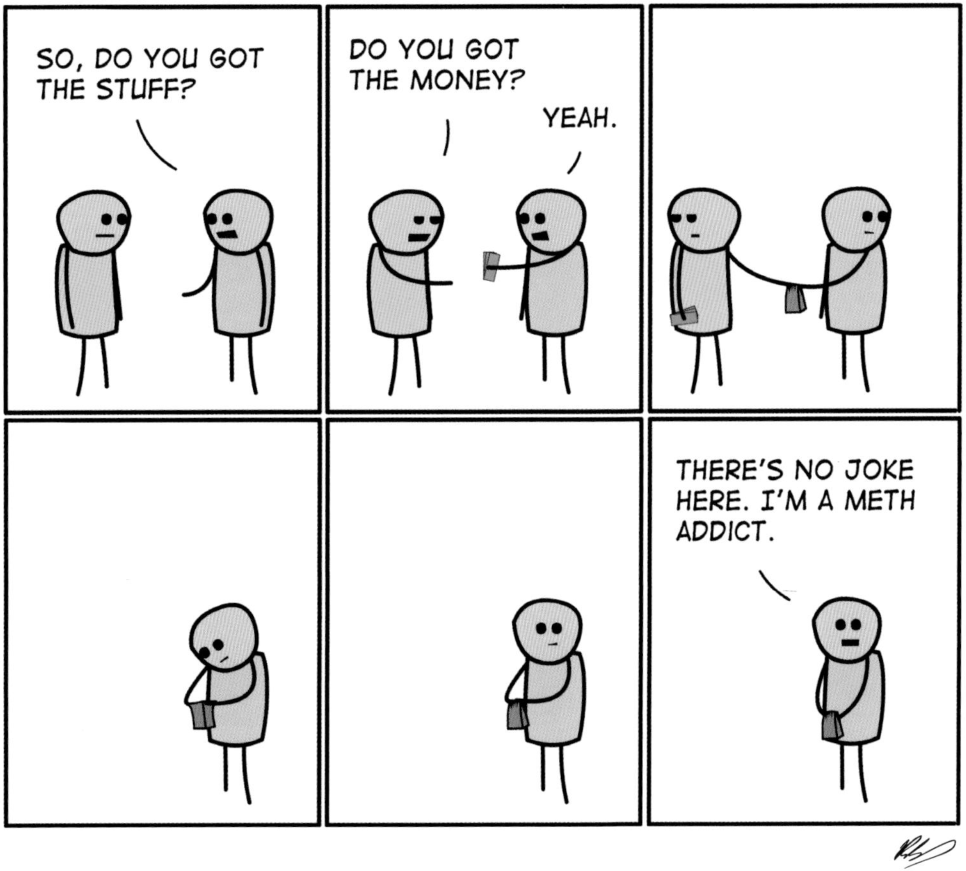
SO, DO YOU GOT THE STUFF?
DO YOU GOT THE MONEY?
YEAH.
THERE'S NO JOKE HERE. I'M A METH ADDICT.

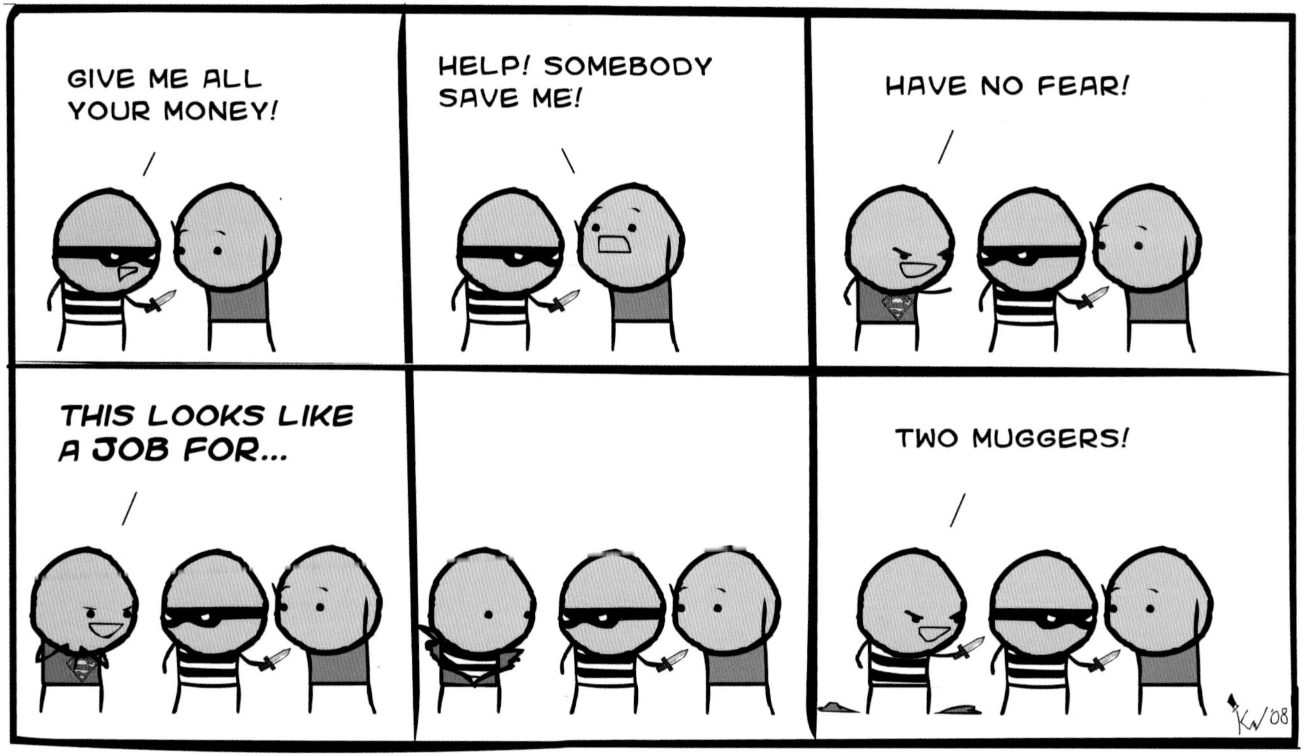
GIVE ME ALL YOUR MONEY!
HELP! SOMEBODY SAVE ME!
HAVE NO FEAR!
THIS LOOKS LIKE A JOB FOR...
TWO MUGGERS!
KW '08

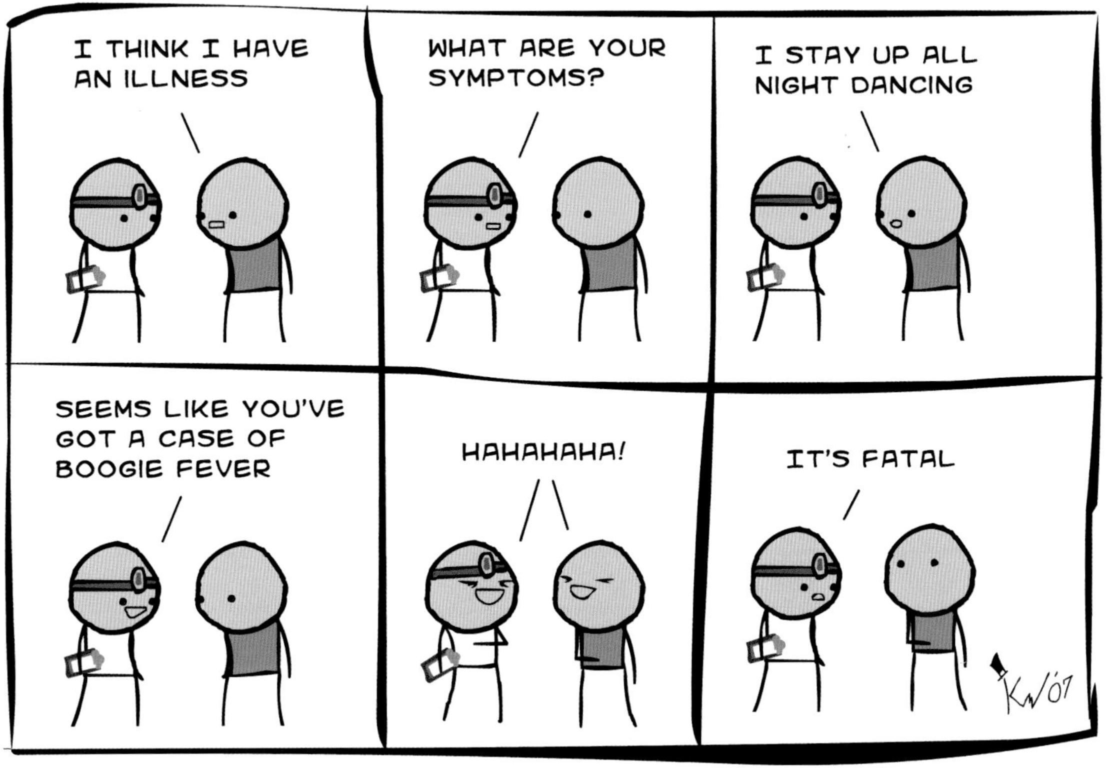
I THINK I HAVE AN ILLNESS
WHAT ARE YOUR SYMPTOMS?
I STAY UP ALL NIGHT DANCING
SEEMS LIKE YOU'VE GOT A CASE OF BOOGIE FEVER
HAHAHAHA!
IT'S FATAL
KW '07

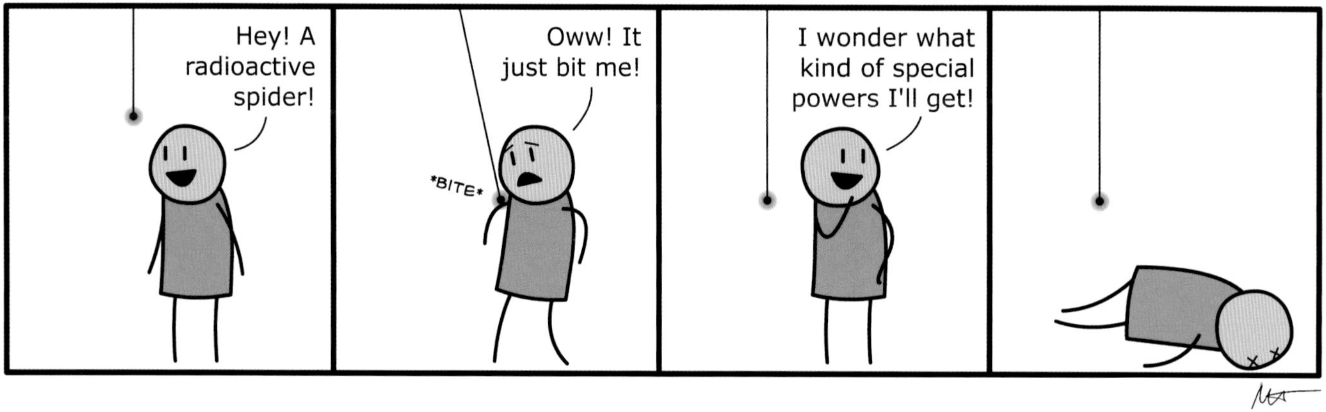
Hey! A radioactive spider!
Oww! It just bit me!
BITE
I wonder what kind of special powers I'll get!

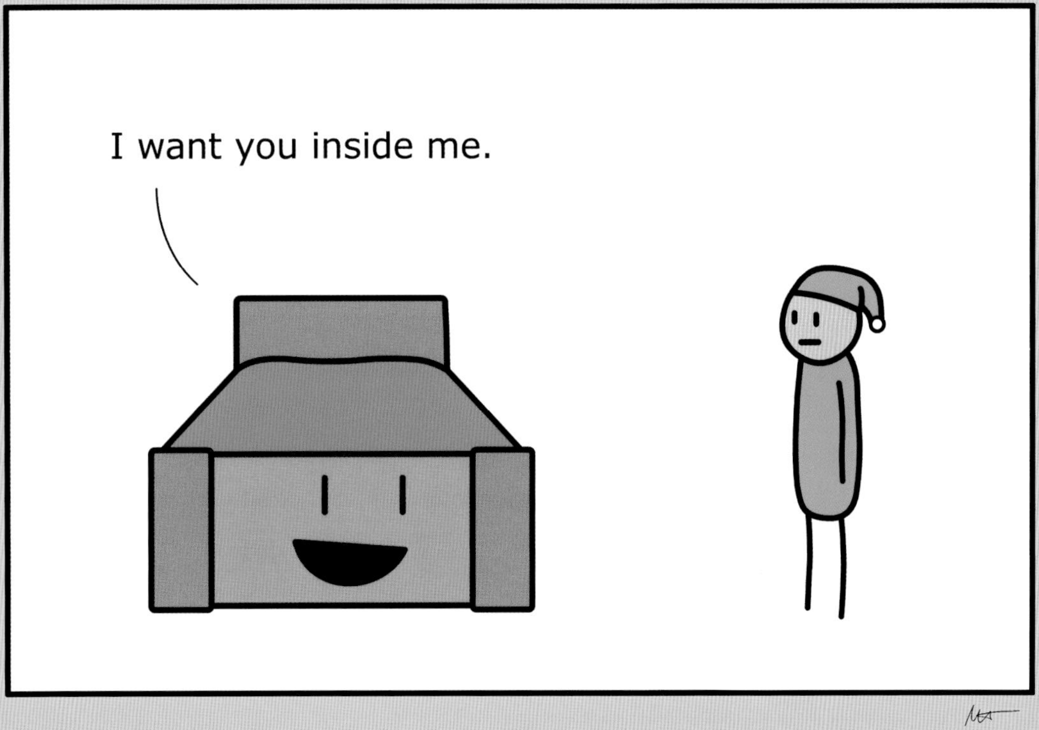
I want you inside me.

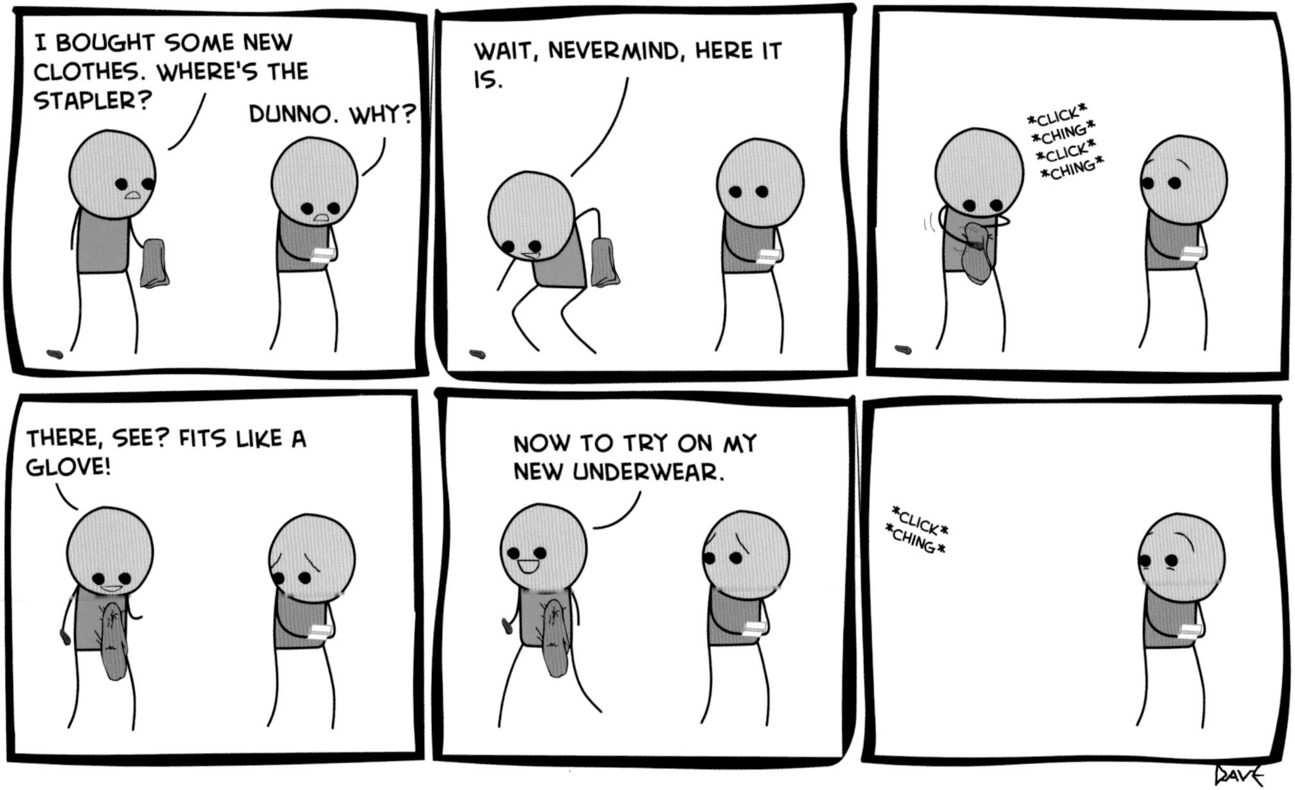
I BOUGHT SOME NEW CLOTHES. WHERE'S THE STAPLER?
DUNNO. WHY?
WAIT, NEVERMIND, HERE IT IS.
CLICK *CHING* *CLICK* *CHING*
THERE, SEE? FITS LIKE A GLOVE!
NOW TO TRY ON MY NEW UNDERWEAR.
CLICK *CHING*
DAVE

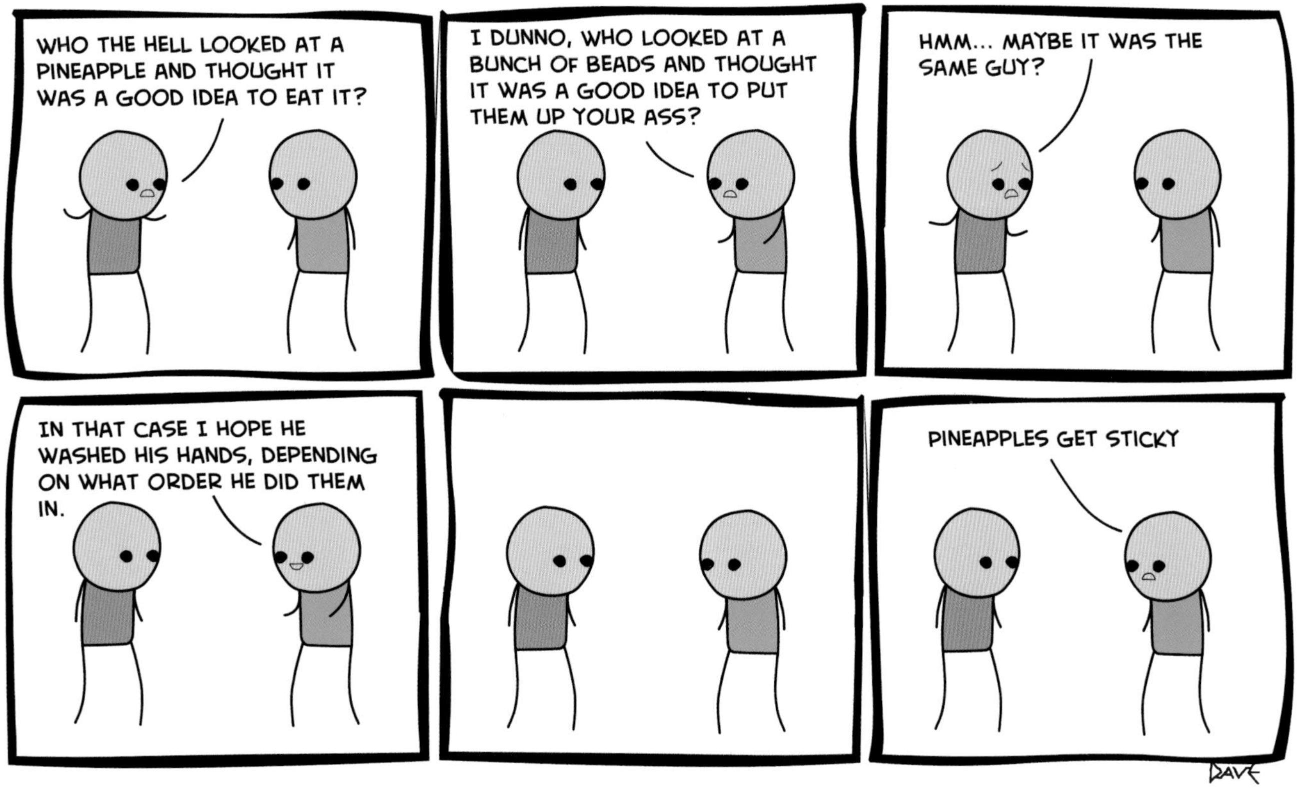
WHO THE HELL LOOKED AT A PINEAPPLE AND THOUGHT IT WAS A GOOD IDEA TO EAT IT?
I DUNNO, WHO LOOKED AT A BUNCH OF BEADS AND THOUGHT IT WAS A GOOD IDEA TO PUT THEM UP YOUR ASS?
HMM... MAYBE IT WAS THE SAME GUY?
IN THAT CASE I HOPE HE WASHED HIS HANDS, DEPENDING ON WHAT ORDER HE DID THEM IN.
PINEAPPLES GET STICKY
DAVE

IS THAT YOUR DOG?
YEAH. SOMETIMES I DRESS HIM IN A FUNNY LITTLE CLOWN COSTUME.
ARE THOSE BURN MARKS?
SOMETIMES I MAKE HIM JUMP THROUGH LITTLE BURNING HOOPS.
I THINK HE'S DEAD.
HE DIED DOING WHAT I LOVE.

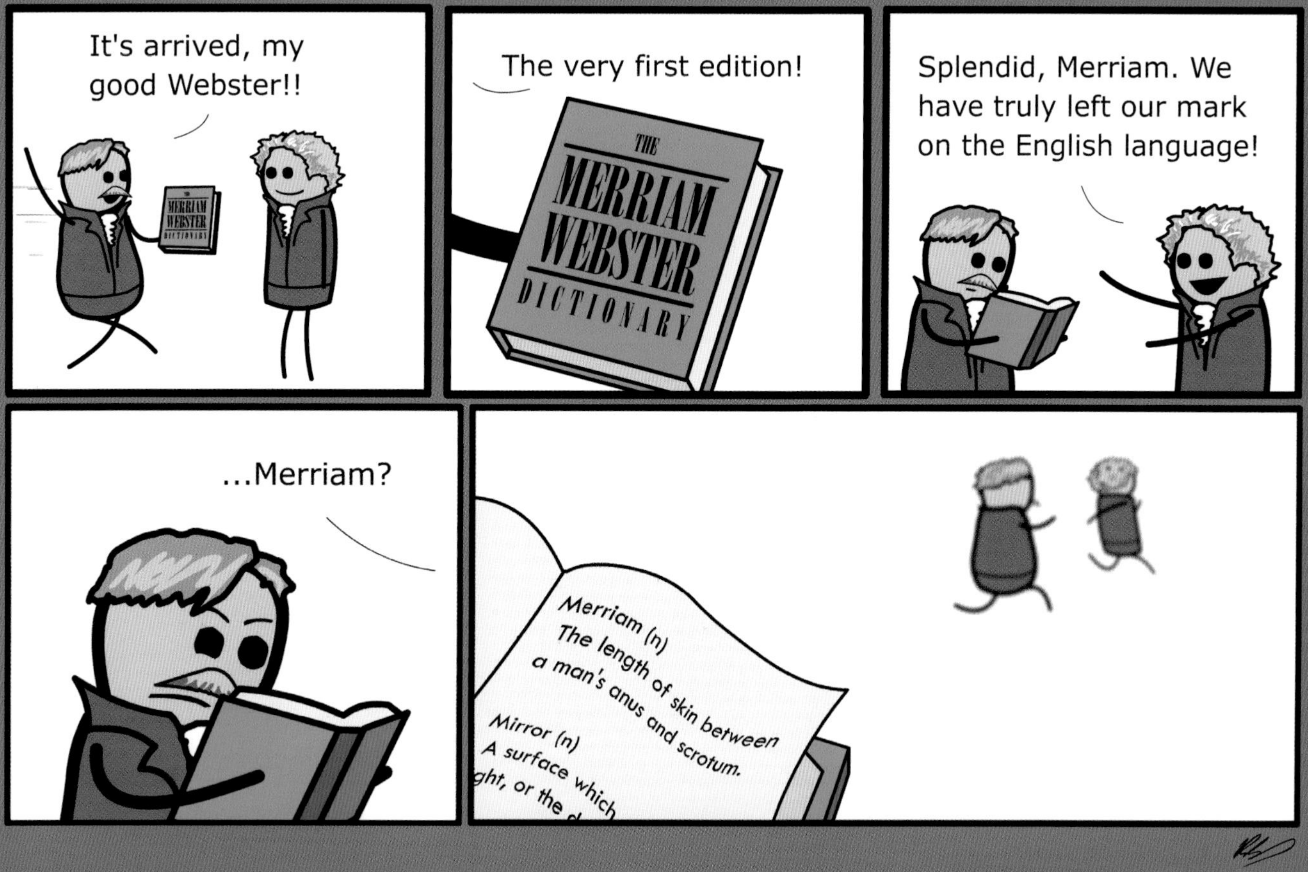
It's arrived, my good Webster!!
The very first edition!
THE MERRIAM WEBSTER DICTIONARY
Splendid, Merriam. We have truly left our mark on the English language!
...Merriam?
Merriam (n)
The length of skin between a man's anus and scrotum.
Mirror (n)
A surface which

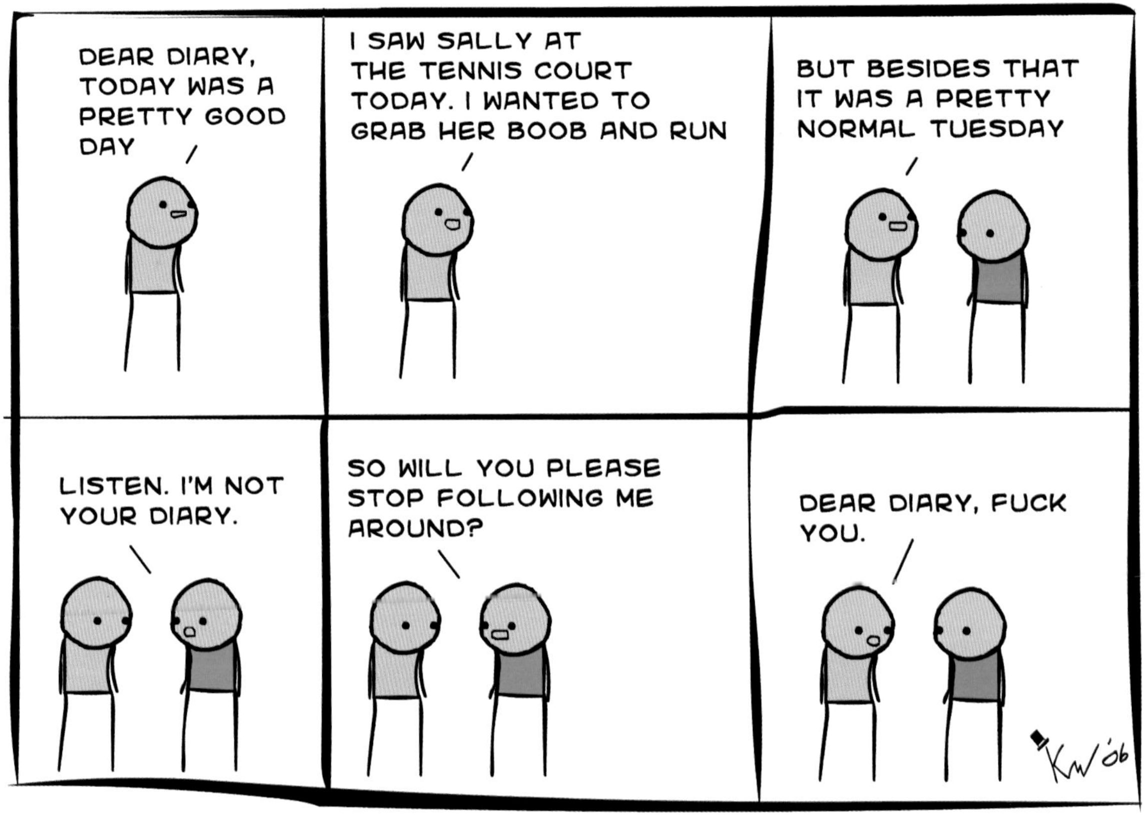
DEAR DIARY, TODAY WAS A PRETTY GOOD DAY
I SAW SALLY AT THE TENNIS COURT TODAY. I WANTED TO GRAB HER BOOB AND RUN
BUT BESIDES THAT IT WAS A PRETTY NORMAL TUESDAY
LISTEN. I'M NOT YOUR DIARY.
SO WILL YOU PLEASE STOP FOLLOWING ME AROUND?
DEAR DIARY, FUCK YOU.
KW '06

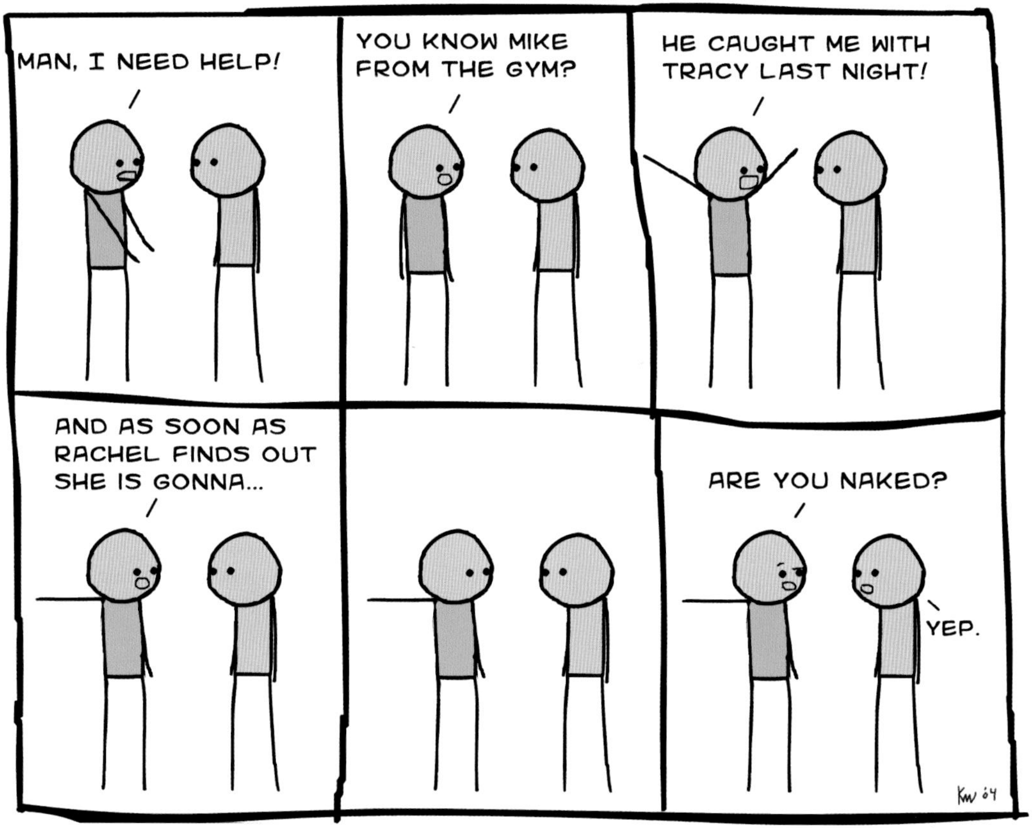
MAN, I NEED HELP!
YOU KNOW MIKE FROM THE GYM?
HE CAUGHT ME WITH TRACY LAST NIGHT!
AND AS SOON AS RACHEL FINDS OUT SHE IS GONNA...
ARE YOU NAKED?
YEP.
KW '04

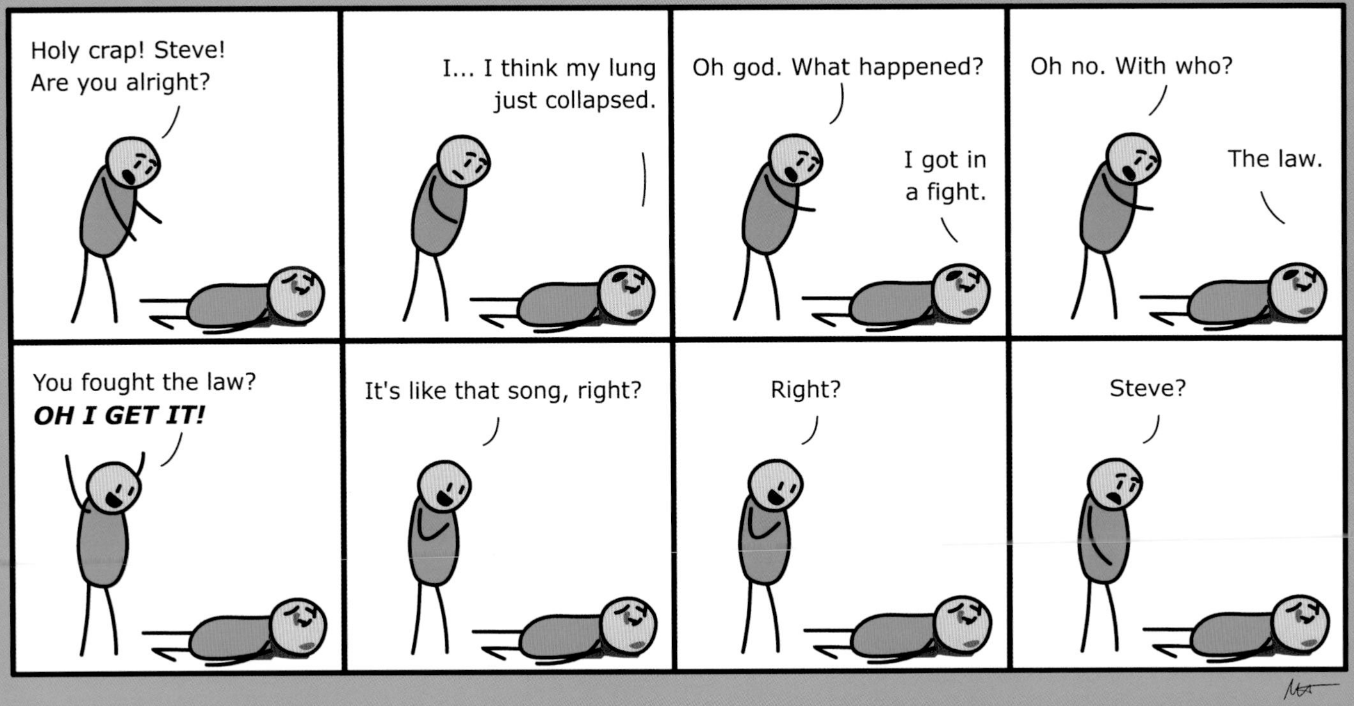
Holy crap! Steve! Are you alright?
I... I think my lung just collapsed.
Oh god. What happened?
I got in a fight.
Oh no. With who?
The law.
You fought the law? OH I GET IT!
It's like that song, right?
Right?
Steve?

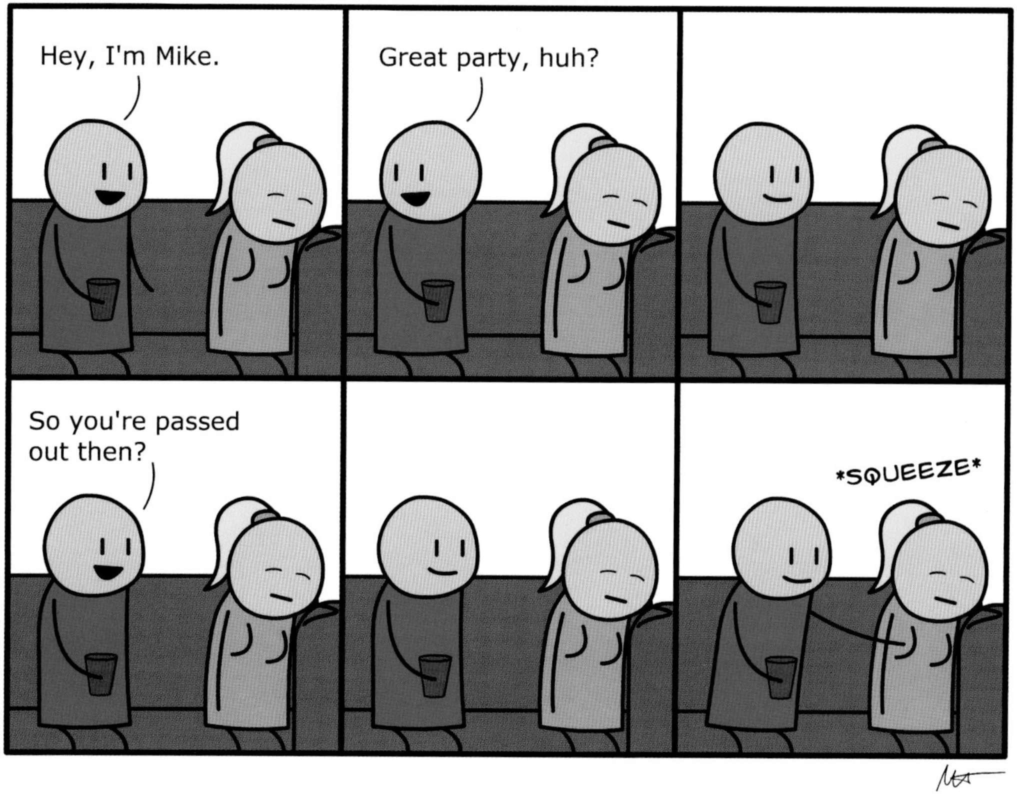
Hey, I'm Mike.
Great party, huh?
So you're passed out then?
SQUEEZE

WAYS TO FUCK WITH PEOPLE #3425 - MAKE THEIR BURGERS LOOK DISAPPOINTED

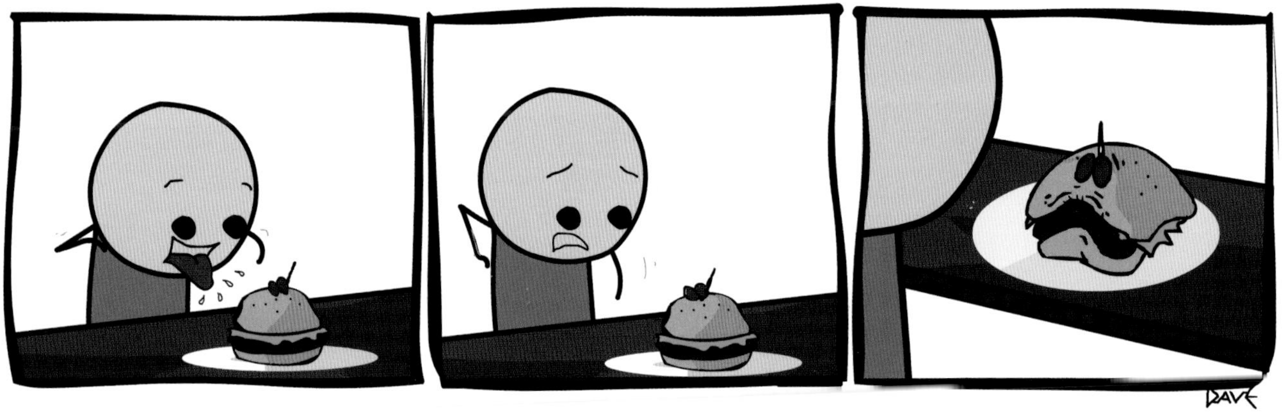
DAVE

DADDY LOOK! THAT MEAN DOG'S HURTING MY CAT!
HEY YOU DUMB MUTT, WHY DON'T YOU PICK ON SOMEONE YOUR OWN SIZE?
STUPID, STUPID, STUPID...
DAVE

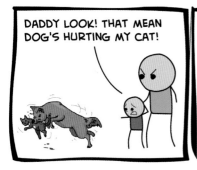

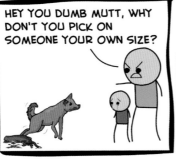

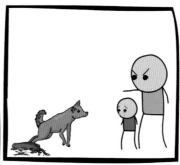

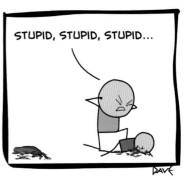

DID YOU HEAR?
TONY JUST DIED.
TONY?? OH GOD...
NO... I DIDN'T GET A CHANCE TO TELL HIM.
TELL HIM WHAT?
THAT I SPILLED ARSENIC IN HIS ORANGE JUICE.

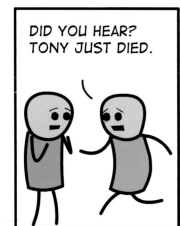

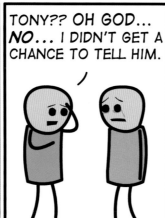

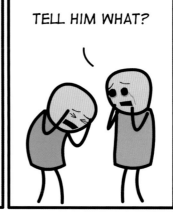

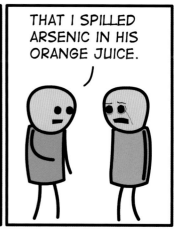

THIS CARNIVAL RULES! CHECK OUT THE COTTON CANDY BOOTH!
I ALREADY WENT TO THE DUNKING BOOTH AND THE FACE-PAINTING BOOTH!
JUST STAY AWAY FROM THE JOHN WILKES BOOTH.

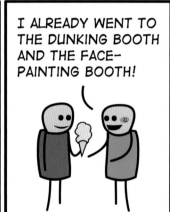

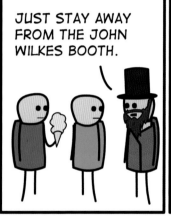

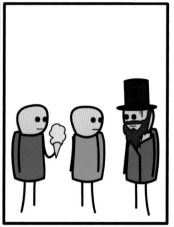

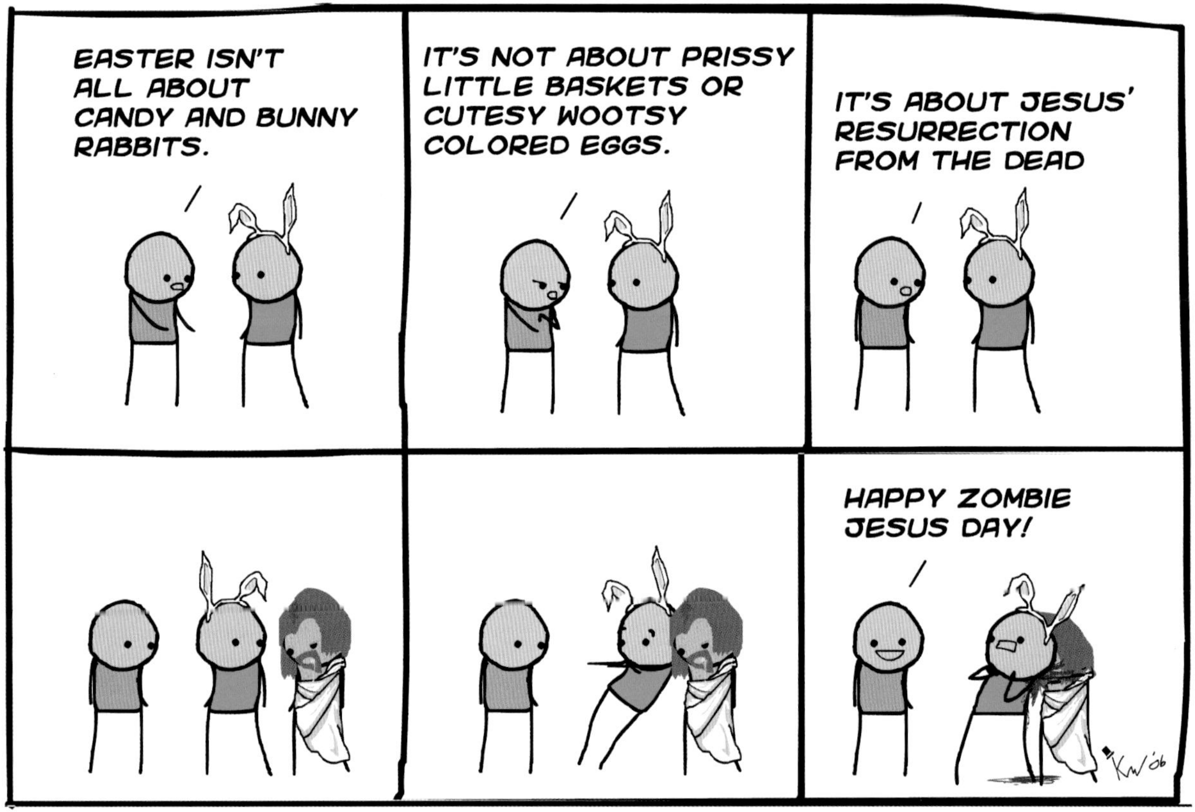
EASTER ISN'T ALL ABOUT CANDY AND BUNNY RABBITS.
IT'S NOT ABOUT PRISSY LITTLE BASKETS OR CUTESY WOOTSY COLORED EGGS.
IT'S ABOUT JESUS' RESURRECTION FROM THE DEAD
HAPPY ZOMBIE JESUS DAY!
KW '06

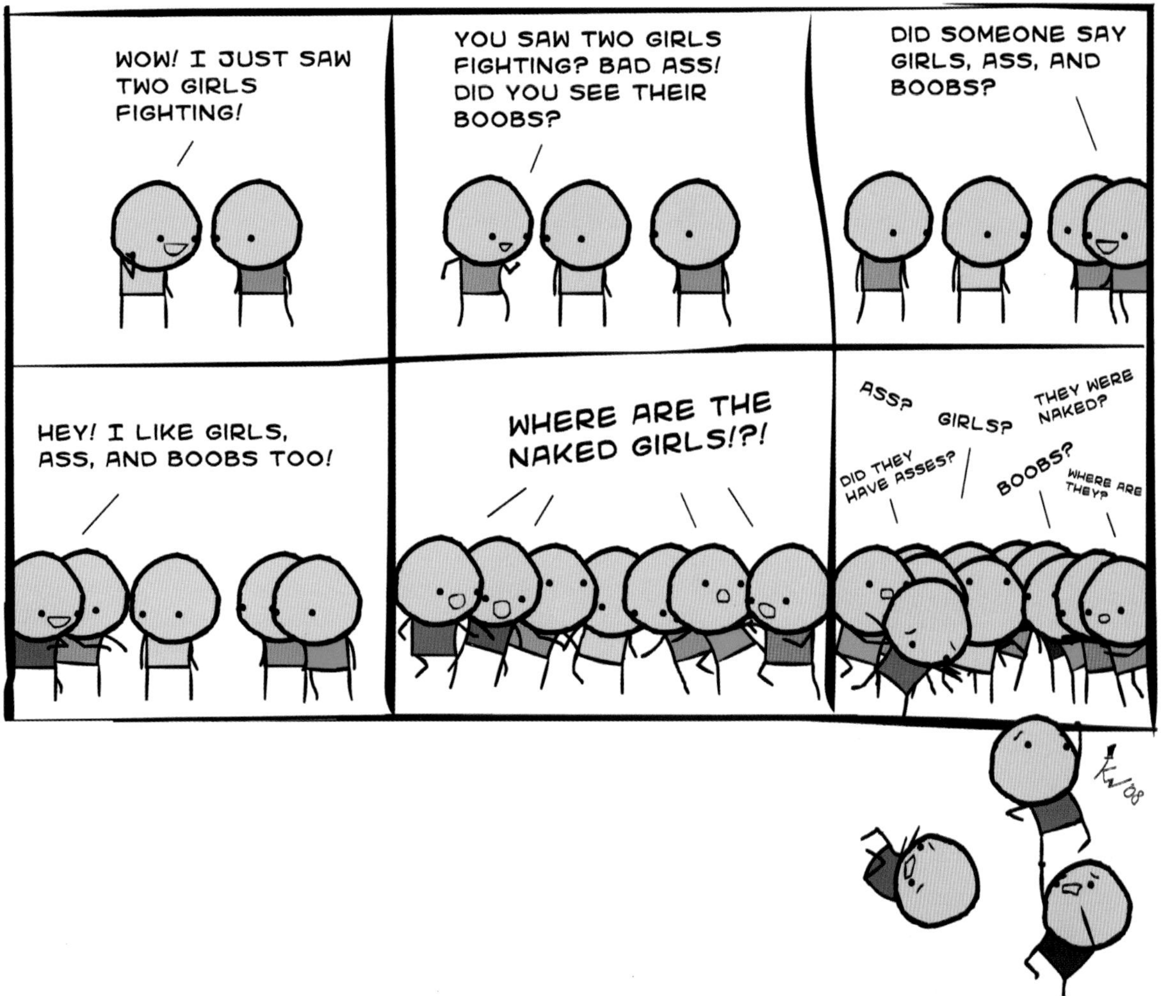
WOW! I JUST SAW TWO GIRLS FIGHTING!
YOU SAW TWO GIRLS FIGHTING? BAD ASS! DID YOU SEE THEIR BOOBS?
DID SOMEONE SAY GIRLS, ASS, AND BOOBS?
HEY! I LIKE GIRLS, ASS, AND BOOBS TOO!
WHERE ARE THE NAKED GIRLS!?!
ASS?
GIRLS?
THEY WERE NAKED?
DID THEY HAVE ASSES?
BOOBS?
WHERE ARE THEY?

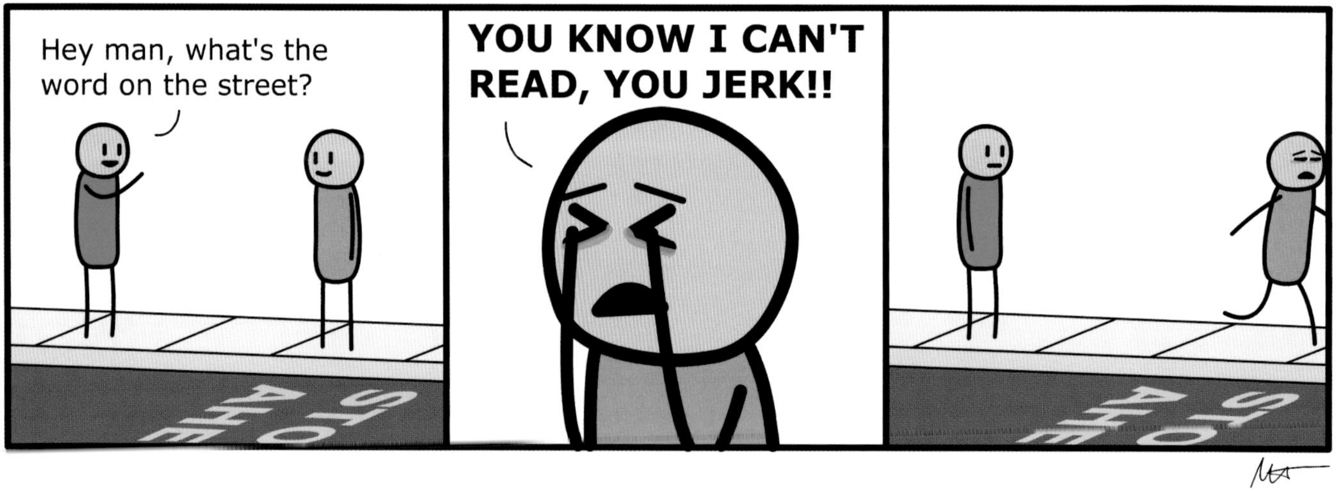
Hey man, what's the word on the street?
YOU KNOW I CAN'T READ, YOU JERK!!

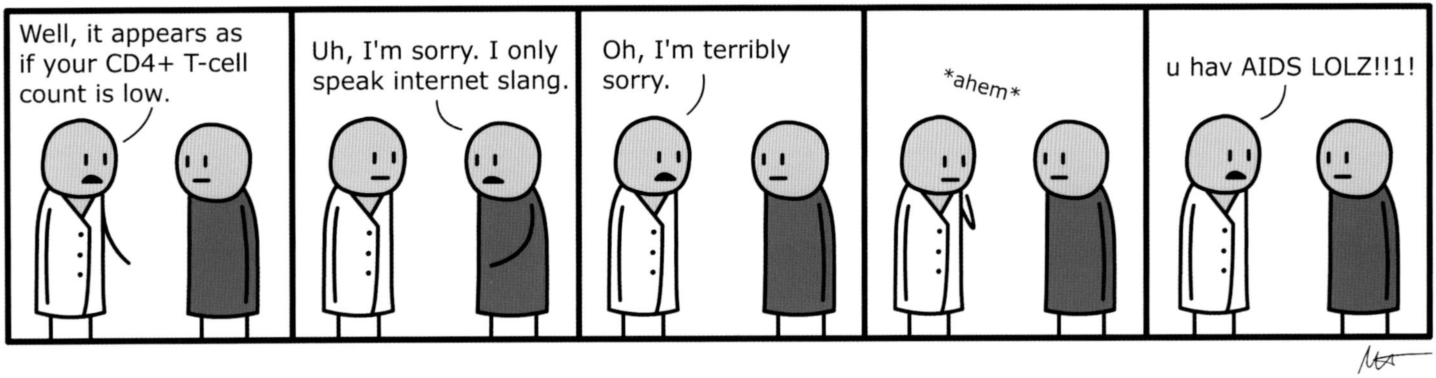
Well, it appears as if your CD4+ T-cell count is low.
Uh, I'm sorry. I only speak internet slang.
Oh, I'm terribly sorry.
ahem
u hav AIDS LOLZ!!1!

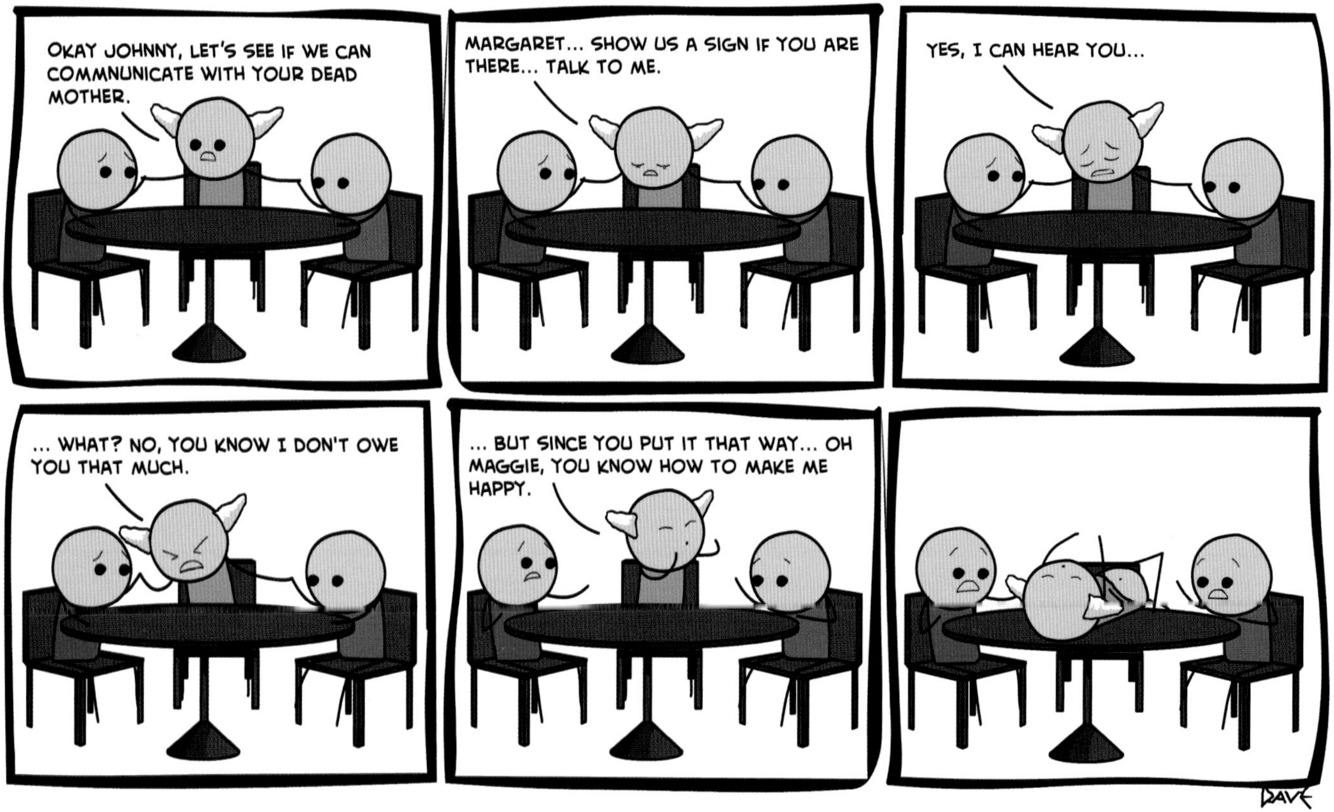
OKAY JOHNNY, LET'S SEE IF WE CAN COMMNUNICATE WITH YOUR DEAD MOTHER.
MARGARET... SHOW US A SIGN IF YOU ARE THERE... TALK TO ME.
YES, I CAN HEAR YOU...
... WHAT? NO, YOU KNOW I DON'T OWE YOU THAT MUCH.
... BUT SINCE YOU PUT IT THAT WAY... OH MAGGIE, YOU KNOW HOW TO MAKE ME HAPPY.
DAVE

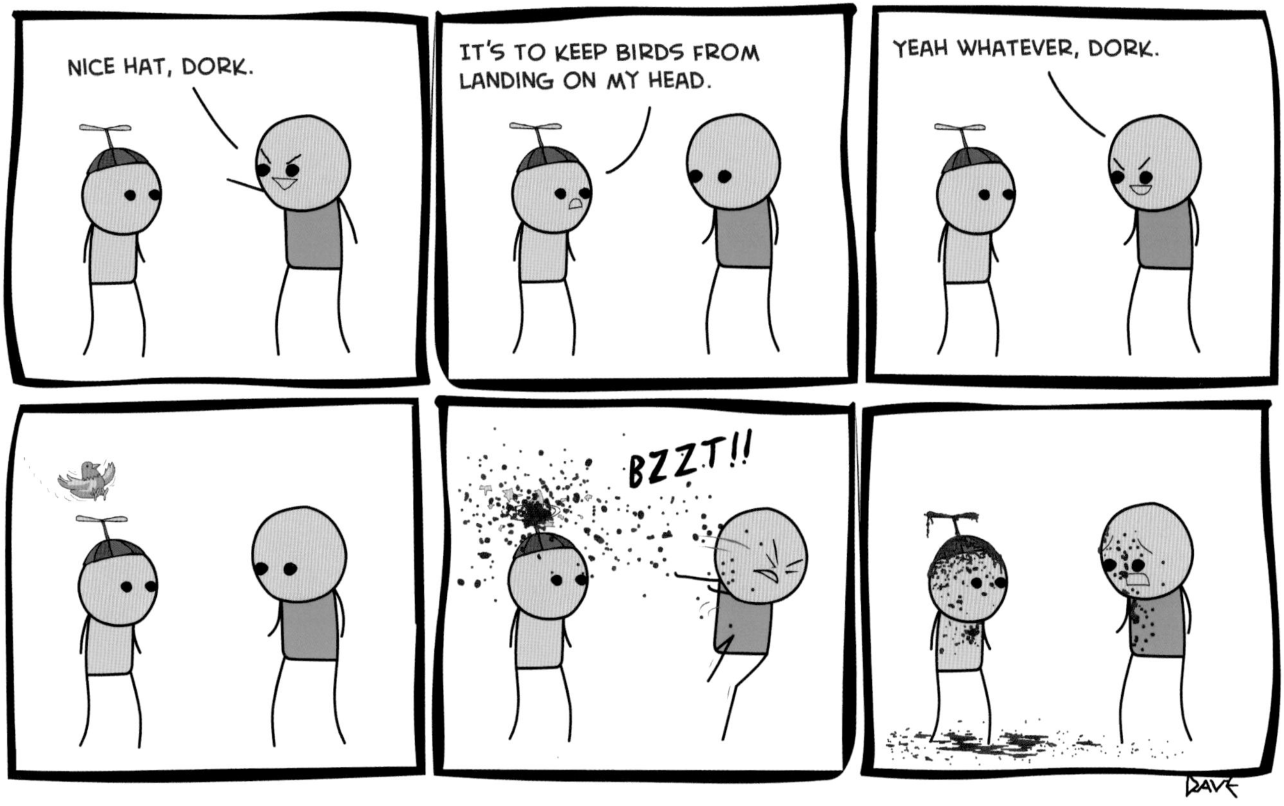
NICE HAT, DORK.
IT'S TO KEEP BIRDS FROM LANDING ON MY HEAD.
YEAH WHATEVER, DORK.
BZZT!!
DAVE

HEY, STROBEL WANTS TO KNOW IF WE WANNA-
HAHAHA HAHA!!!
DUDE... HE HAS CLOWN SYNDROME.

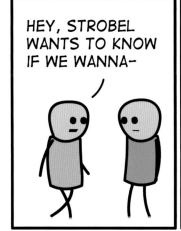

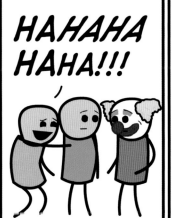

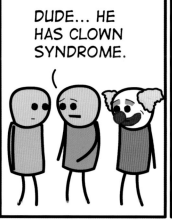

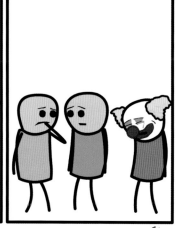

SORRY, STRANGER, BUT I'M THE ONLY SHERIFF IN THIS HERE TOWN.
I KNOW. I'M JUST THE GRAMMAR SHERIFF.
THAT DON'T SEEM LIKE NO KINDA SHERIFF TO ME.

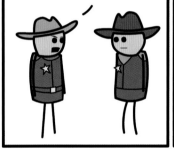

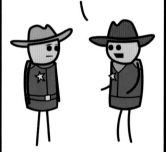

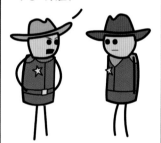

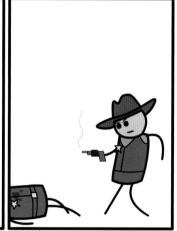

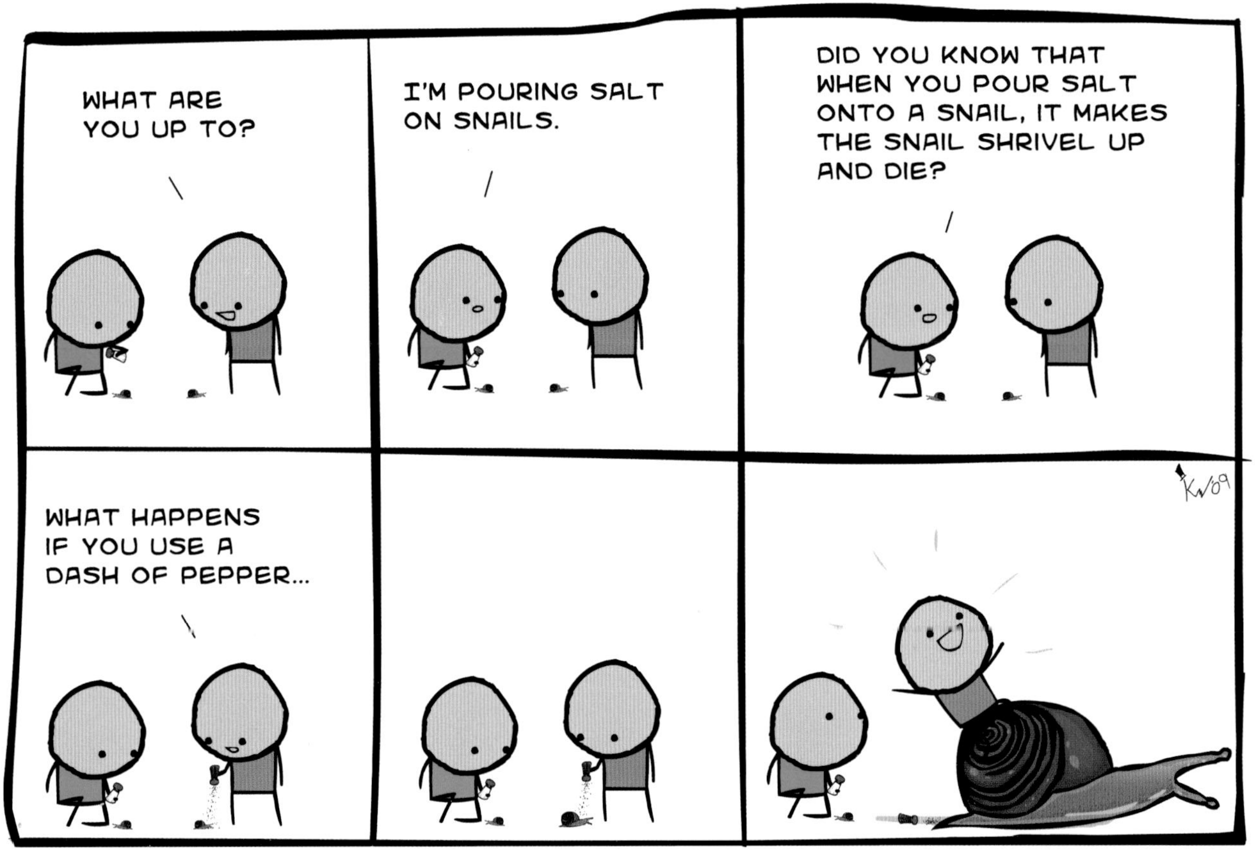
WHAT ARE YOU UP TO?
I'M POURING SALT ON SNAILS.
DID YOU KNOW THAT WHEN YOU POUR SALT ONTO A SNAIL, IT MAKES THE SNAIL SHRIVEL UP AND DIE?
WHAT HAPPENS IF YOU USE A DASH OF PEPPER...
KW'09

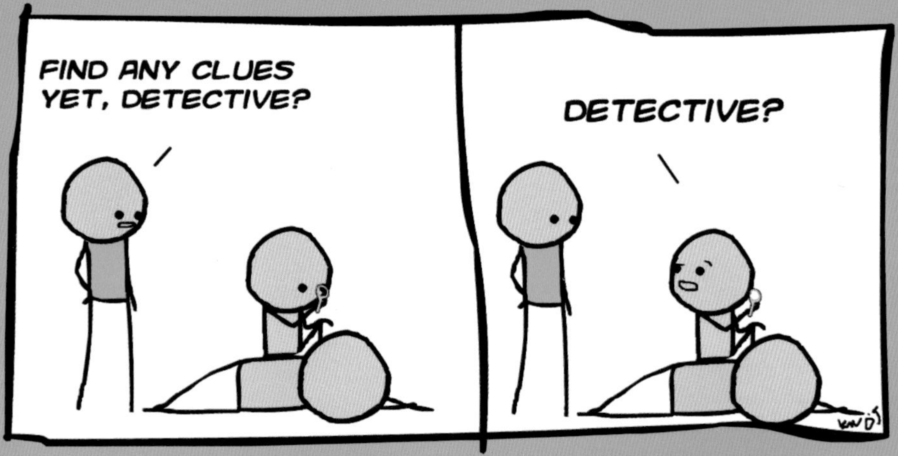
FIND ANY CLUES
YET, DETECTIVE?
DETECTIVE?

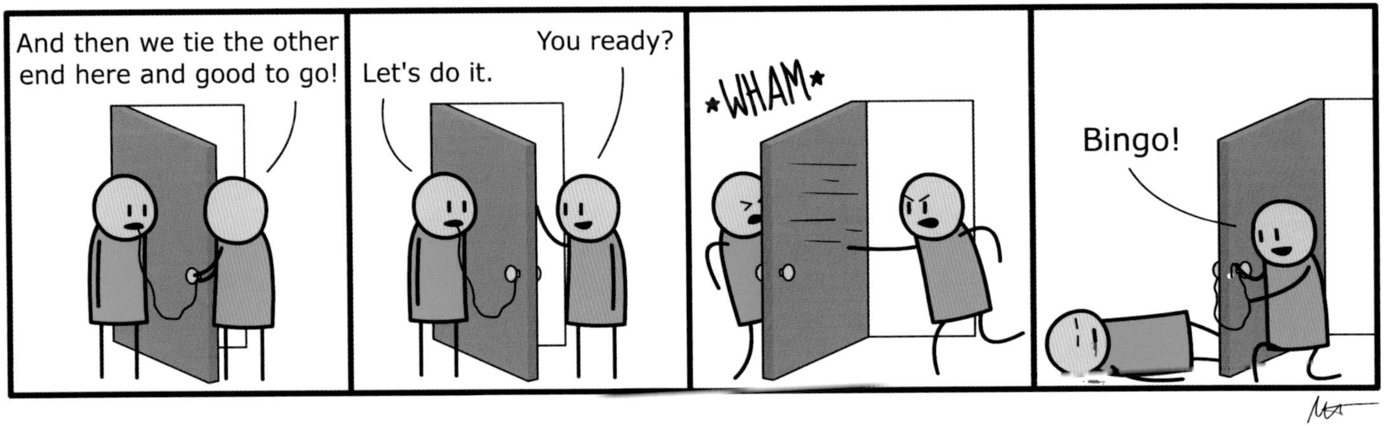
And then we tie the other end here and good to go!
You ready?
Let's do it.
WHAM
Bingo!

COMICS-THAT-90%-OF-THE-GENERAL-PUBLIC-WON'T-UNDERSTAND WEEK

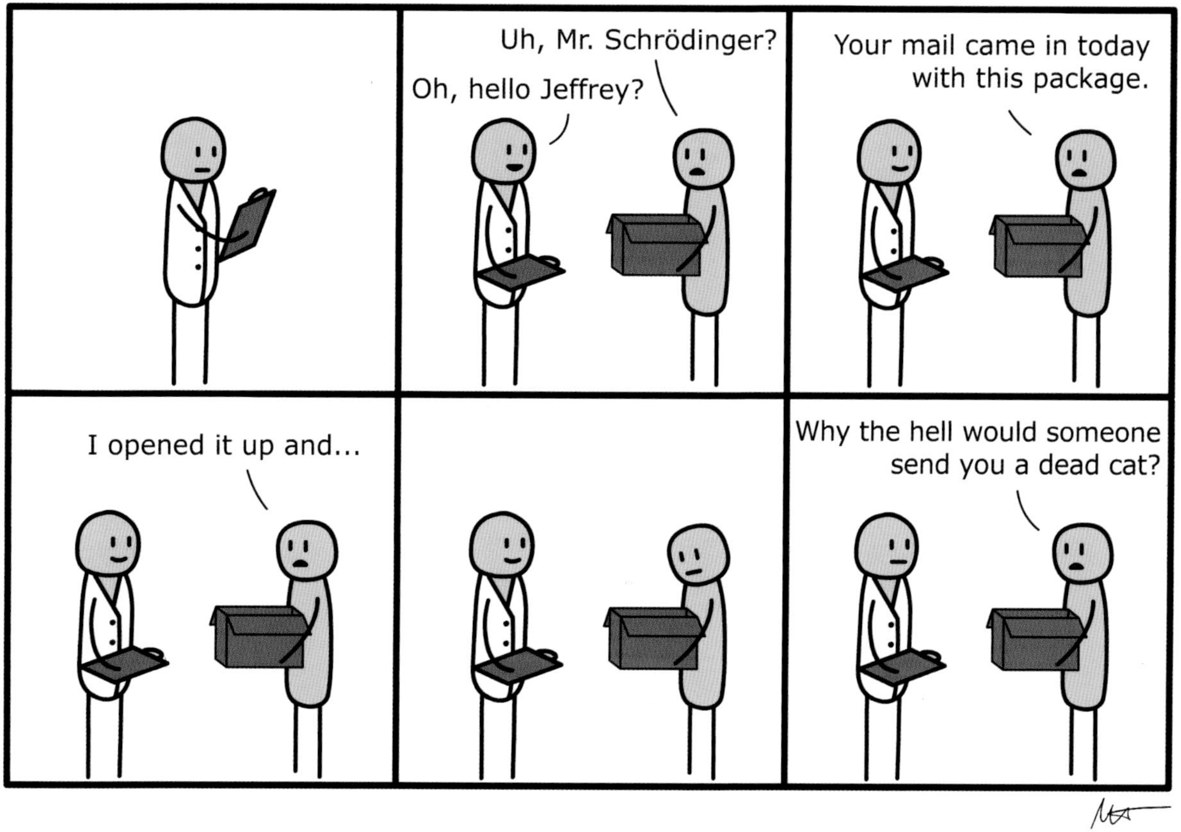
Uh, Mr. Schrödinger?
Oh, hello Jeffrey?
Your mail came in today with this package.
I opened it up and...
Why the hell would someone send you a dead cat?

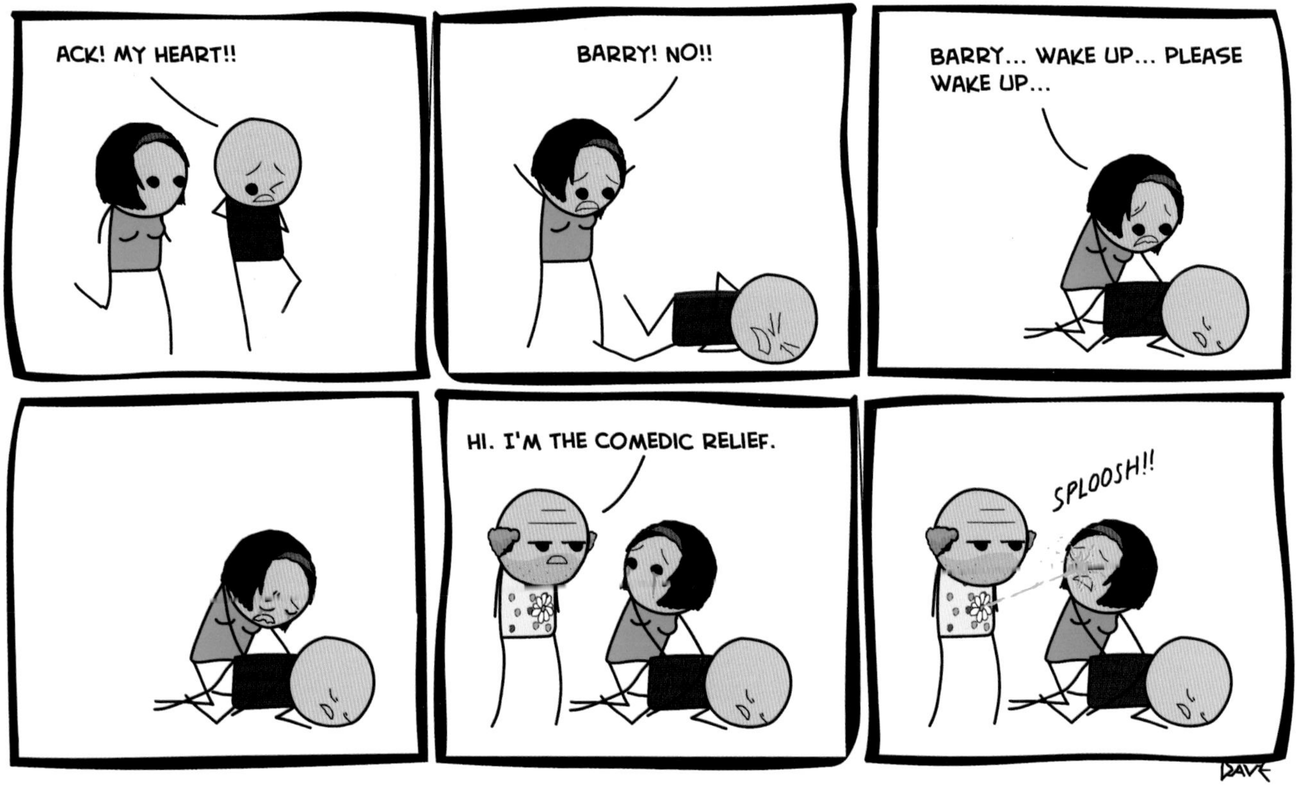
ACK! MY HEART!!
BARRY! NO!!
BARRY... WAKE UP... PLEASE WAKE UP...
HI. I'M THE COMEDIC RELIEF.
SPLOOSH!!
DAVE

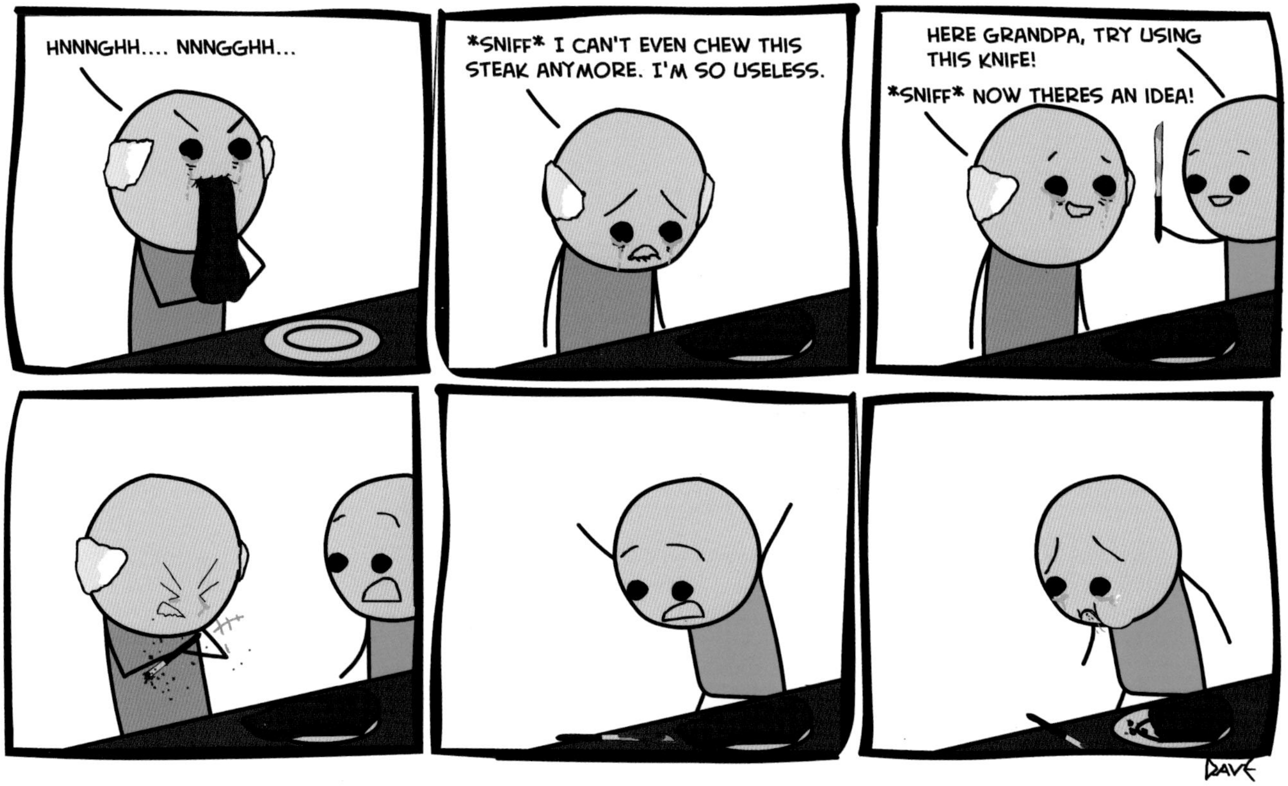
HNNNGHH.... NNNGGHH...
SNIFF I CAN'T EVEN CHEW THIS STEAK ANYMORE. I'M SO USELESS.
HERE GRANDPA, TRY USING THIS KNIFE!
SNIFF NOW THERES AN IDEA!
DAVE

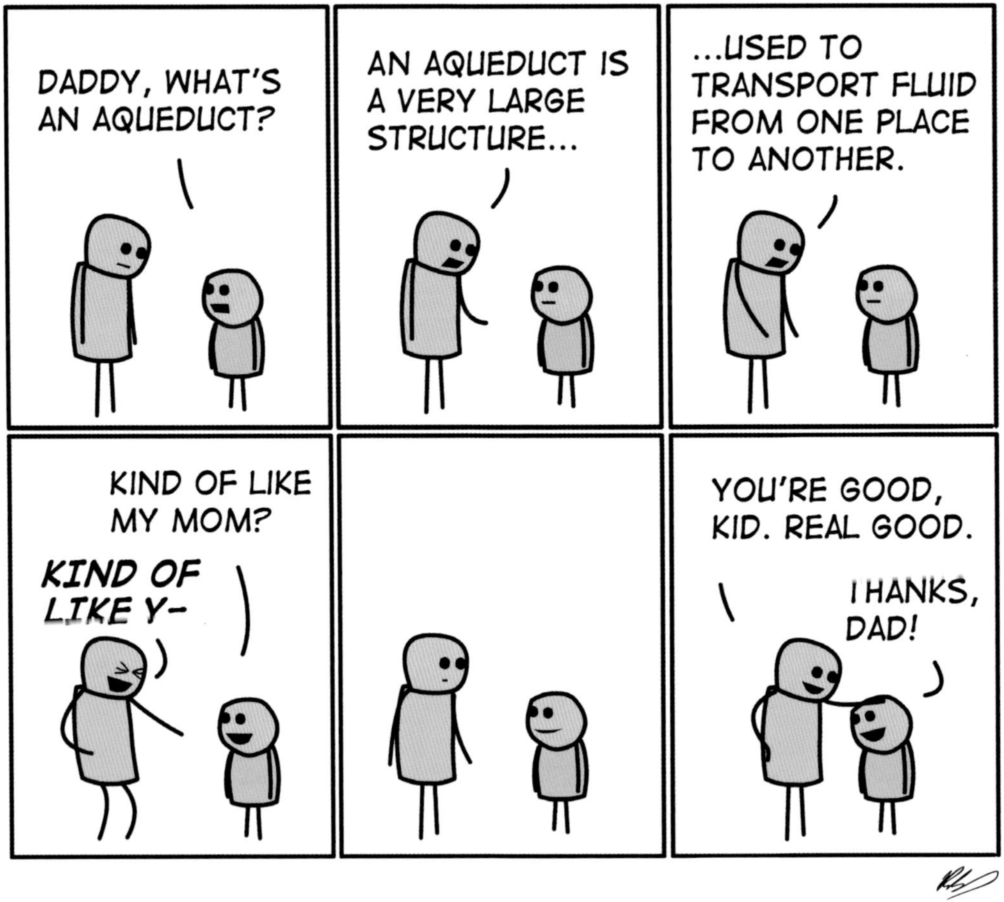
DADDY, WHAT'S AN AQUEDUCT?
AN AQUEDUCT IS A VERY LARGE STRUCTURE...
...USED TO TRANSPORT FLUID FROM ONE PLACE TO ANOTHER.
KIND OF LIKE MY MOM?
KIND OF LIKE Y-
YOU'RE GOOD, KID. REAL GOOD.
THANKS, DAD!

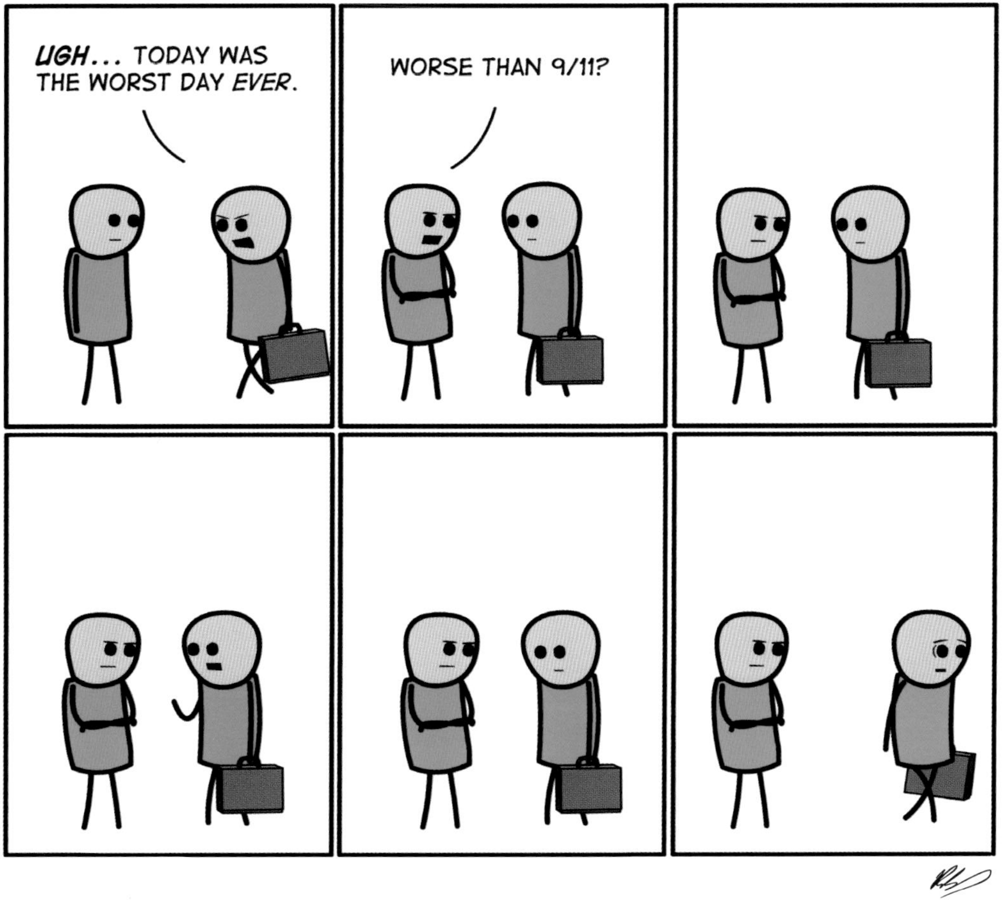

UGH... TODAY WAS THE WORST DAY EVER.
WORSE THAN 9/11?

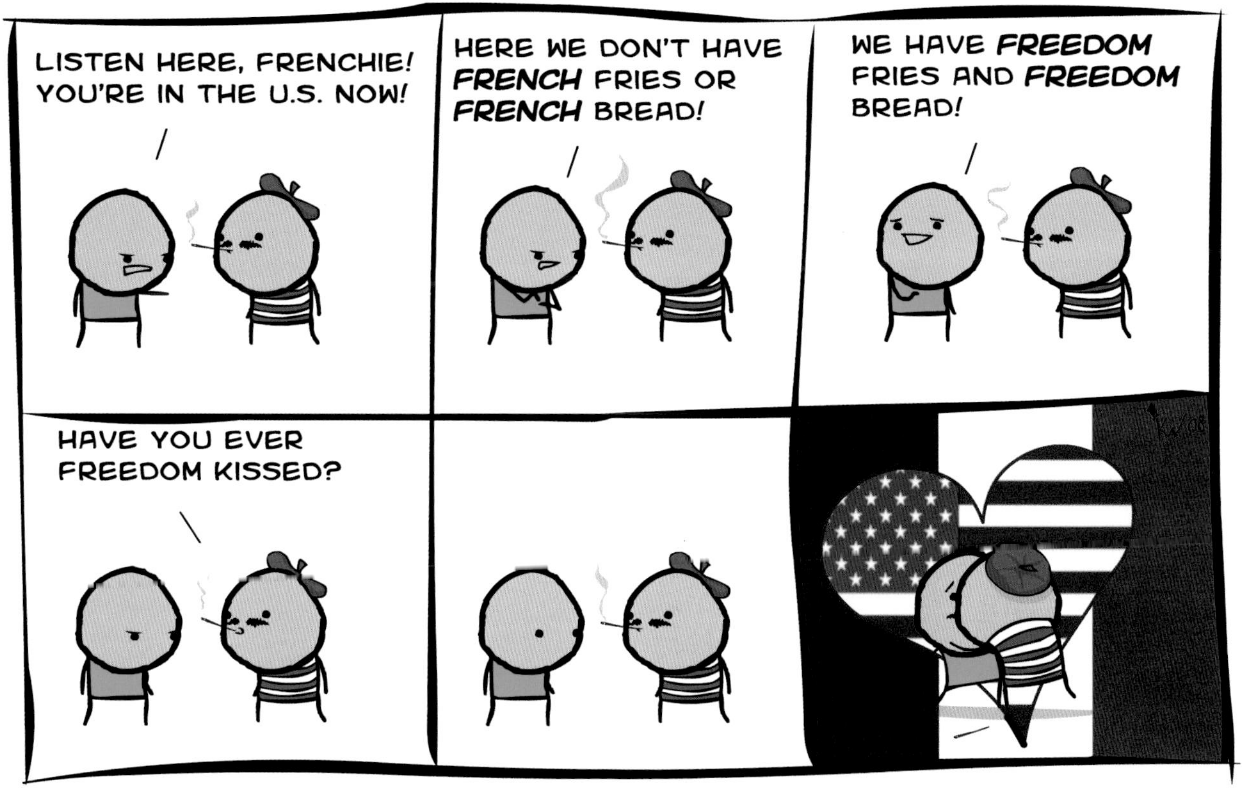
LISTEN HERE, FRENCHIE! YOU'RE IN THE U.S. NOW!
HERE WE DON'T HAVE **FRENCH** FRIES OR **FRENCH** BREAD!
WE HAVE **FREEDOM** FRIES AND **FREEDOM** BREAD!
HAVE YOU EVER FREEDOM KISSED?

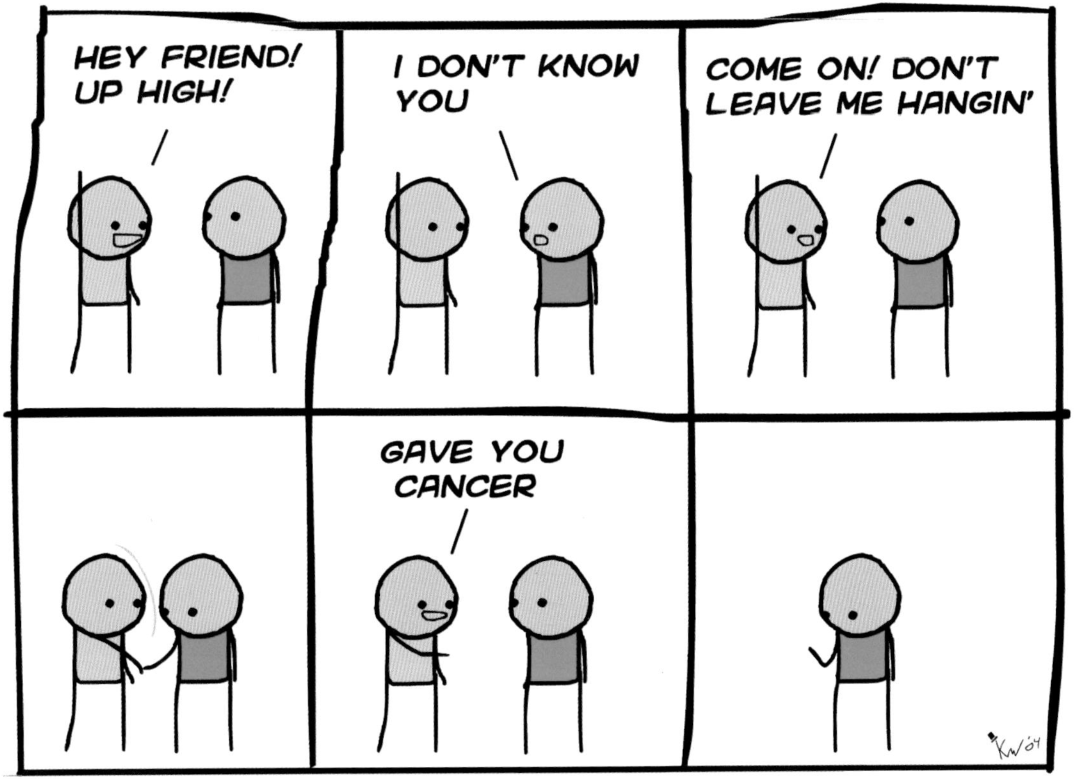
HEY FRIEND! UP HIGH!
I DON'T KNOW YOU
COME ON! DON'T LEAVE ME HANGIN'
GAVE YOU CANCER
KW '04

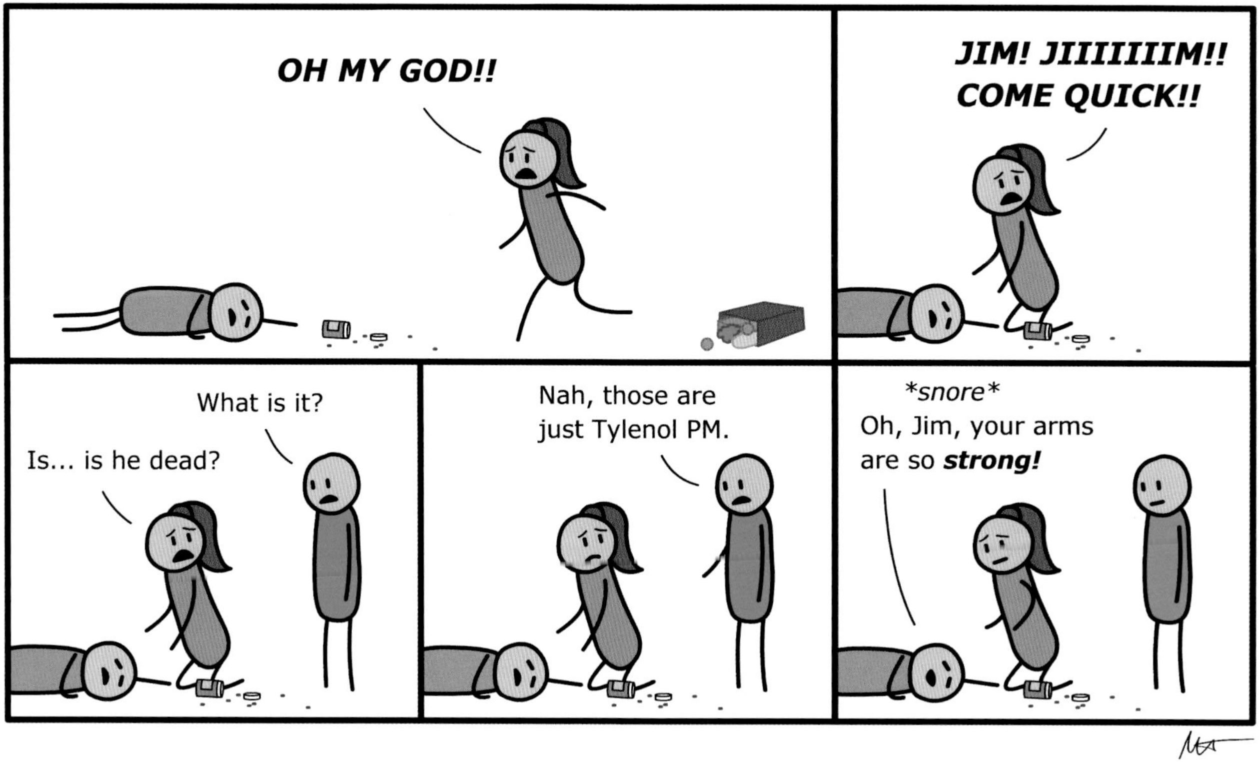
OH MY GOD!!
JIM! JIIIIIIIM!! COME QUICK!!
Is... is he dead?
What is it?
Nah, those are just Tylenol PM.
snore
Oh, Jim, your arms are so **strong!**

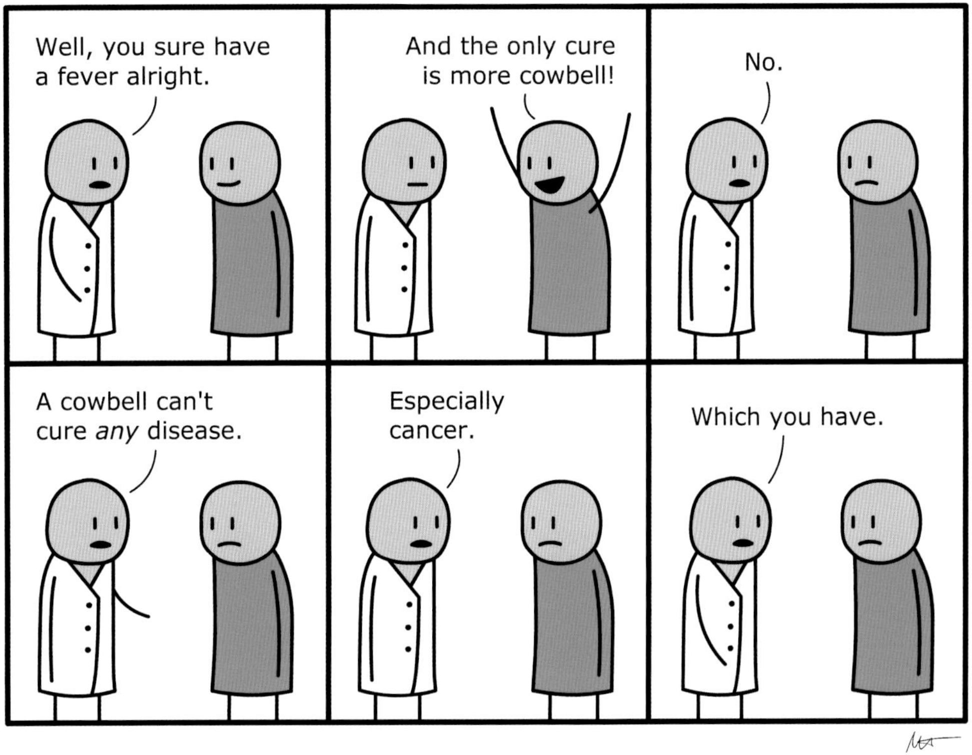
Well, you sure have a fever alright.
And the only cure is more cowbell!
No.
A cowbell can't cure *any* disease.
Especially cancer.
Which you have.

OH, YOU GOT SOME MEAT FOR THE BARBEQUE AFTER ALL, WONDERFUL!
ANYWAY, I'M GOING NOW TO BUY TIMMY A GIFT. MAYBE IT'LL STOP HIM CRYING LIKE HE HAS DONE ALL AFTERNOON.
NOW THAT I MENTION IT, WHERE IS TIMMY?
YOU EVER HEARD OF THE PHRASE "TWO BIRDS ONE STONE?"
DAVE

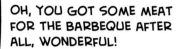

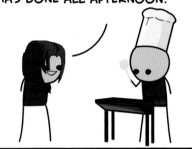

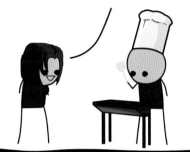

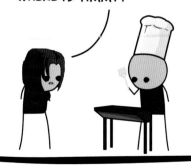

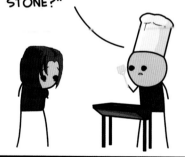

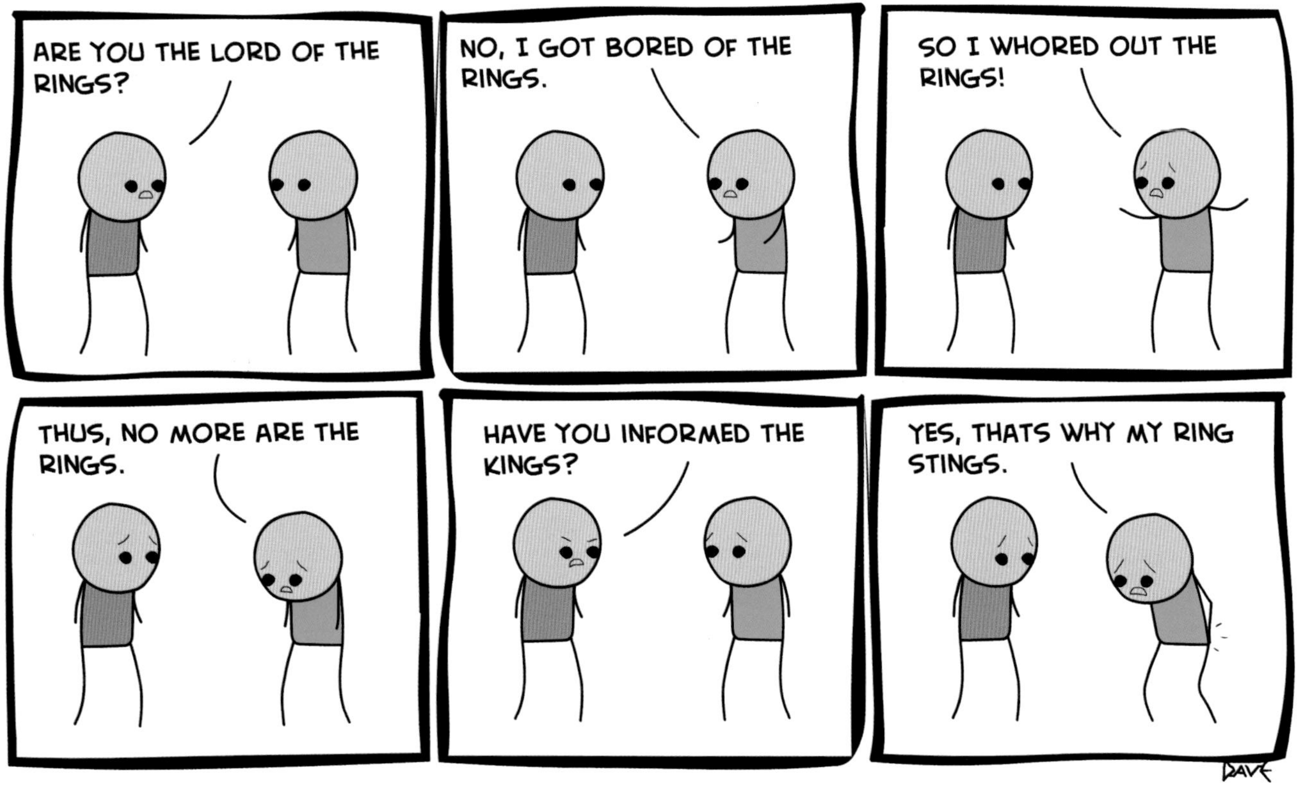
ARE YOU THE LORD OF THE RINGS?
NO, I GOT BORED OF THE RINGS.
SO I WHORED OUT THE RINGS!
THUS, NO MORE ARE THE RINGS.
HAVE YOU INFORMED THE KINGS?
YES, THATS WHY MY RING STINGS.
DAVE

THE NEW ONES

30 Never-Before-Seen Comics...

UNCENSORED.

UNSEEMLY.

UNASHAMED.

MAN, MUSIC THESE DAYS IS PRETTY BAD.
HEH... *THAT'S* AN UNDERSTATEMENT.
NO, THIS IS AN UNDERSTATEMENT.
I DON'T GET IT.
ME EITHER.

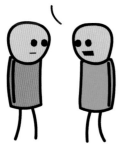

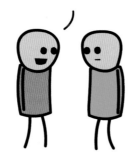

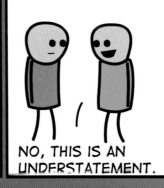

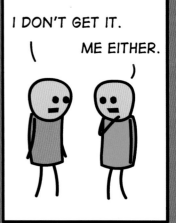

LET'S PLAY A LITTLE GAME, **HOSTAGES**... IT'S CALLED *WHO SHOULD I KILL FIRST?*
ACTUALLY, IT'S "*WHOM* SHOULD I KILL FIRST"

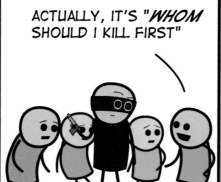

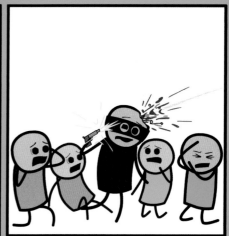

WHAT ARE YOU DOING!? STOP STABBING YOUR GIRLFRIEND!
DON'T WORRY SHE LIKES IT
CHICKS DIG SCARS
KW'09

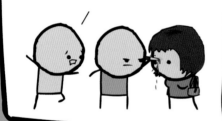

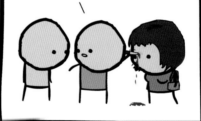

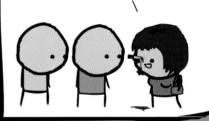

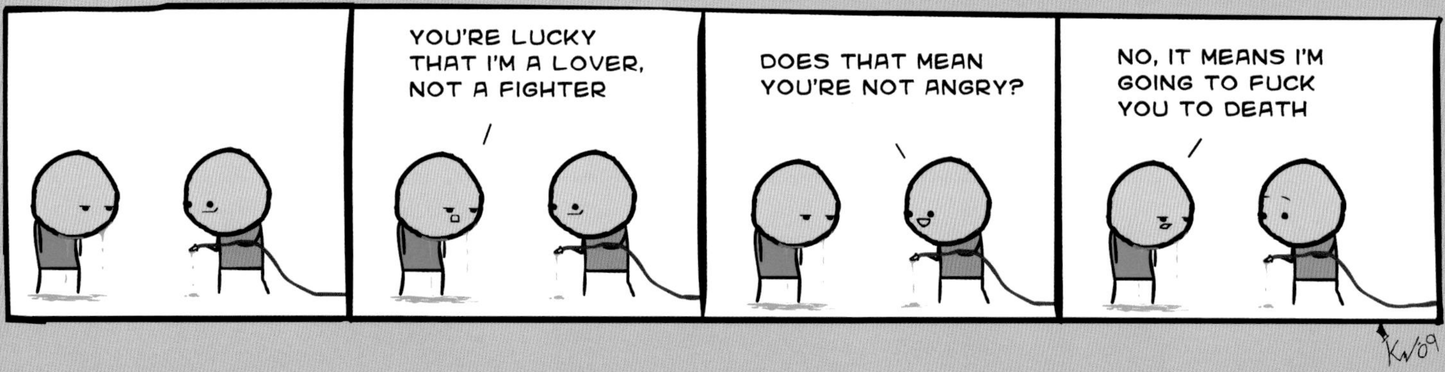
YOU'RE LUCKY THAT I'M A LOVER, NOT A FIGHTER
DOES THAT MEAN YOU'RE NOT ANGRY?
NO, IT MEANS I'M GOING TO FUCK YOU TO DEATH
KW'09

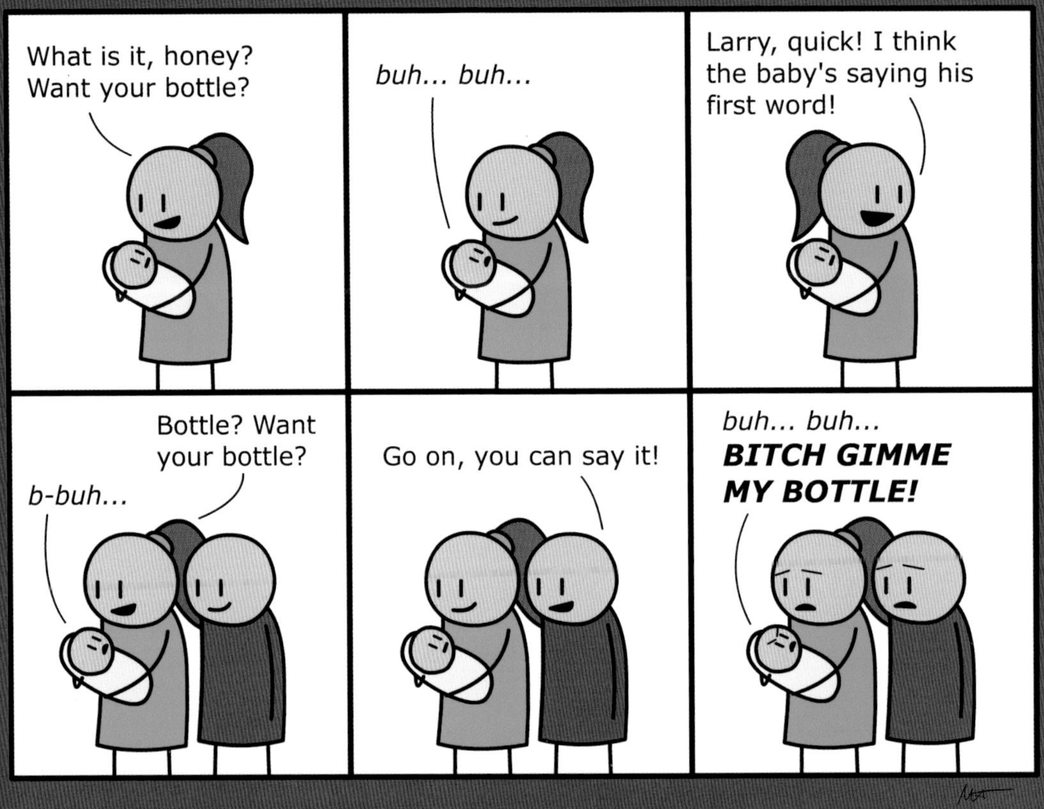
What is it, honey? Want your bottle?
buh... buh...
Larry, quick! I think the baby's saying his first word!
Bottle? Want your bottle?
b-buh...
Go on, you can say it!
buh... buh...
BITCH GIMME MY BOTTLE!

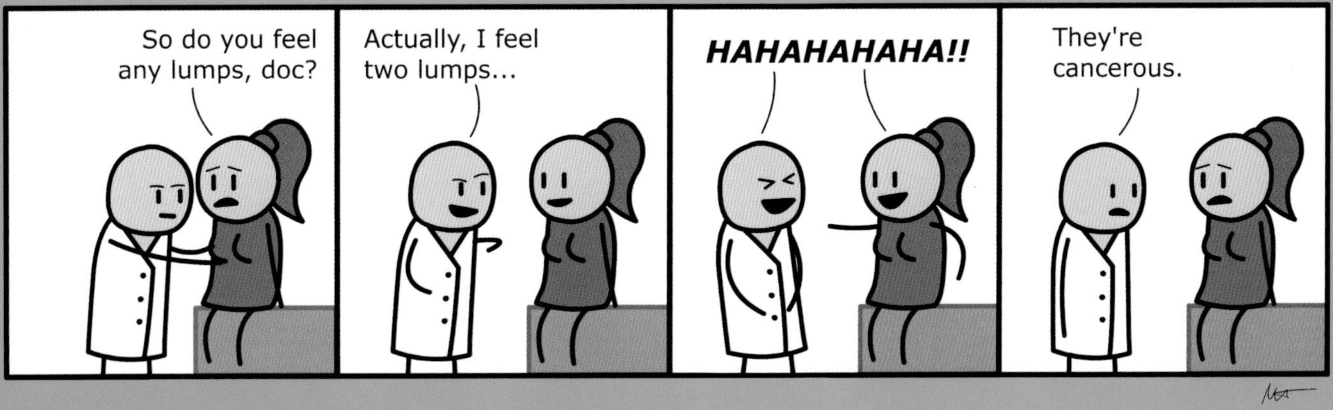
So do you feel any lumps, doc?
Actually, I feel two lumps...
HAHAHAHAHA!!
They're cancerous.

I DIDN'T KNOW WHAT TO DO WITH THIS OLD STOOL...
... SO I TOOK THE LEGS OFF IT, AND IT TURNED OUT TO BE A RATHER FETCHING FRISBEE!
HAH, YOU ONLY FIGURED THAT OUT NOW? THAT RULE APPLIES TO EVERYTHING!
DAVE

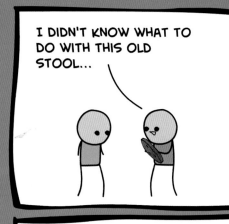

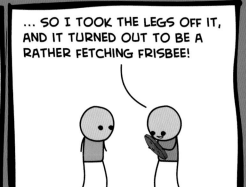

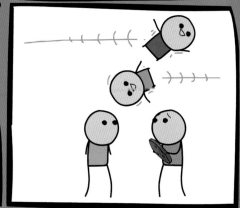

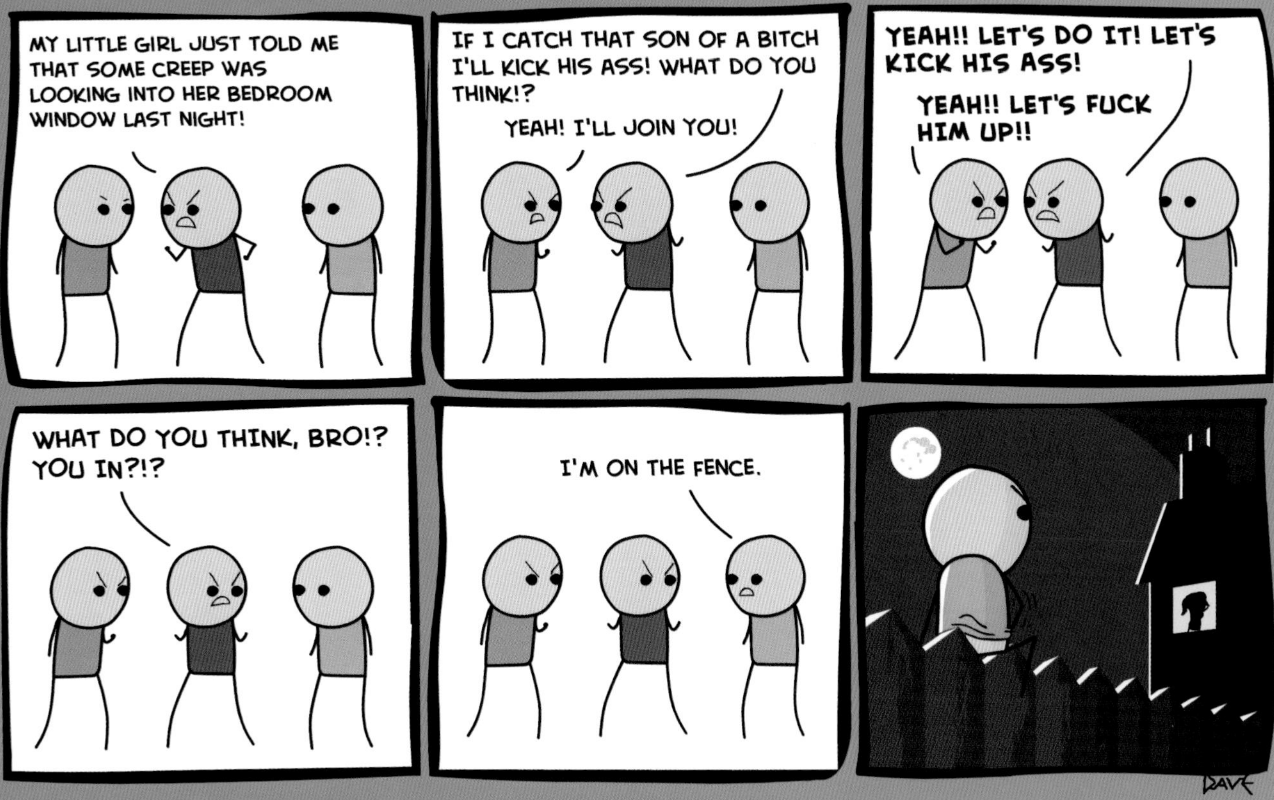
MY LITTLE GIRL JUST TOLD ME THAT SOME CREEP WAS LOOKING INTO HER BEDROOM WINDOW LAST NIGHT!
IF I CATCH THAT SON OF A BITCH I'LL KICK HIS ASS! WHAT DO YOU THINK!?
YEAH! I'LL JOIN YOU!
YEAH!! LET'S DO IT! LET'S KICK HIS ASS!
YEAH!! LET'S FUCK HIM UP!!
WHAT DO YOU THINK, BRO!? YOU IN?!?
I'M ON THE FENCE.
DAVE

WOW... LOOKS LIKE *SOOOME*ONE'S ON A CLEANING BINGE.
SHIT YEAH. I'VE BEEN CLEANING MY BUTT OFF ALL MORNING!
NICE.

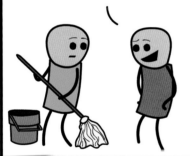

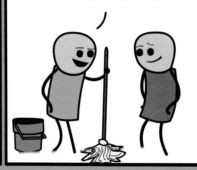

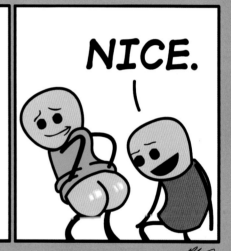

I'M SORRY TO TELL YOU THIS, MA'AM, BUT THERE'S BEEN AN ACCIDENT. YOUR SON IS DEAD.

OH GOD!! NO...

HEH, JUST KIDDING. IT'S OPPOSITE DAY.

IT WAS YOUR DAUGHTER.

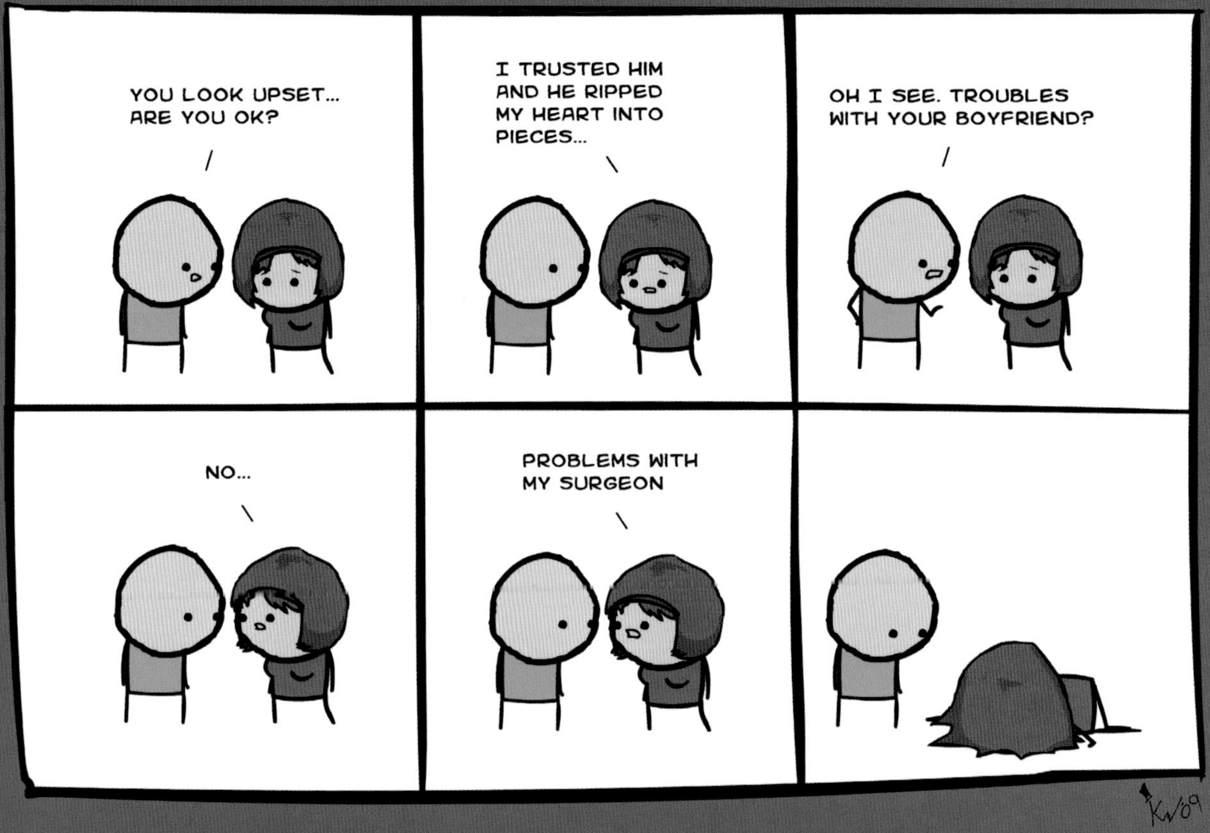
YOU LOOK UPSET... ARE YOU OK?
I TRUSTED HIM AND HE RIPPED MY HEART INTO PIECES...
OH I SEE. TROUBLES WITH YOUR BOYFRIEND?
NO...
PROBLEMS WITH MY SURGEON
KW '09

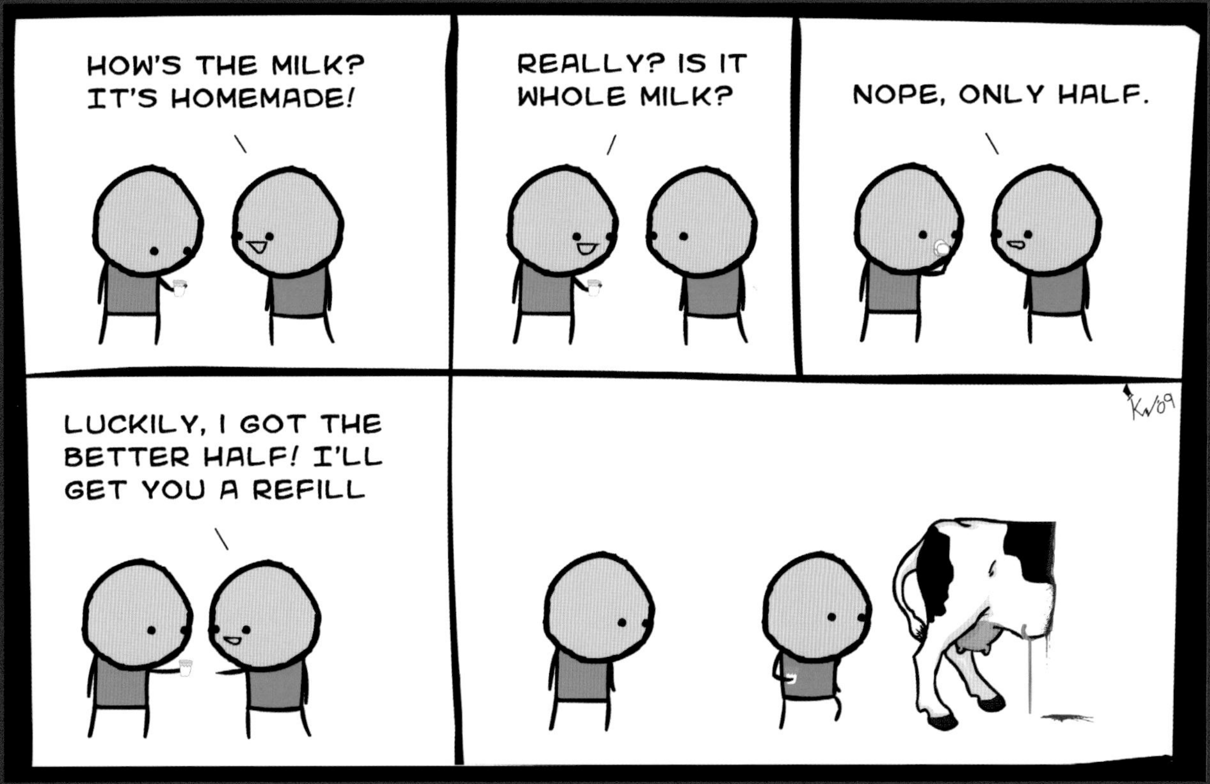
HOW'S THE MILK? IT'S HOMEMADE!
REALLY? IS IT WHOLE MILK?
NOPE, ONLY HALF.
LUCKILY, I GOT THE BETTER HALF! I'LL GET YOU A REFILL
KW'09

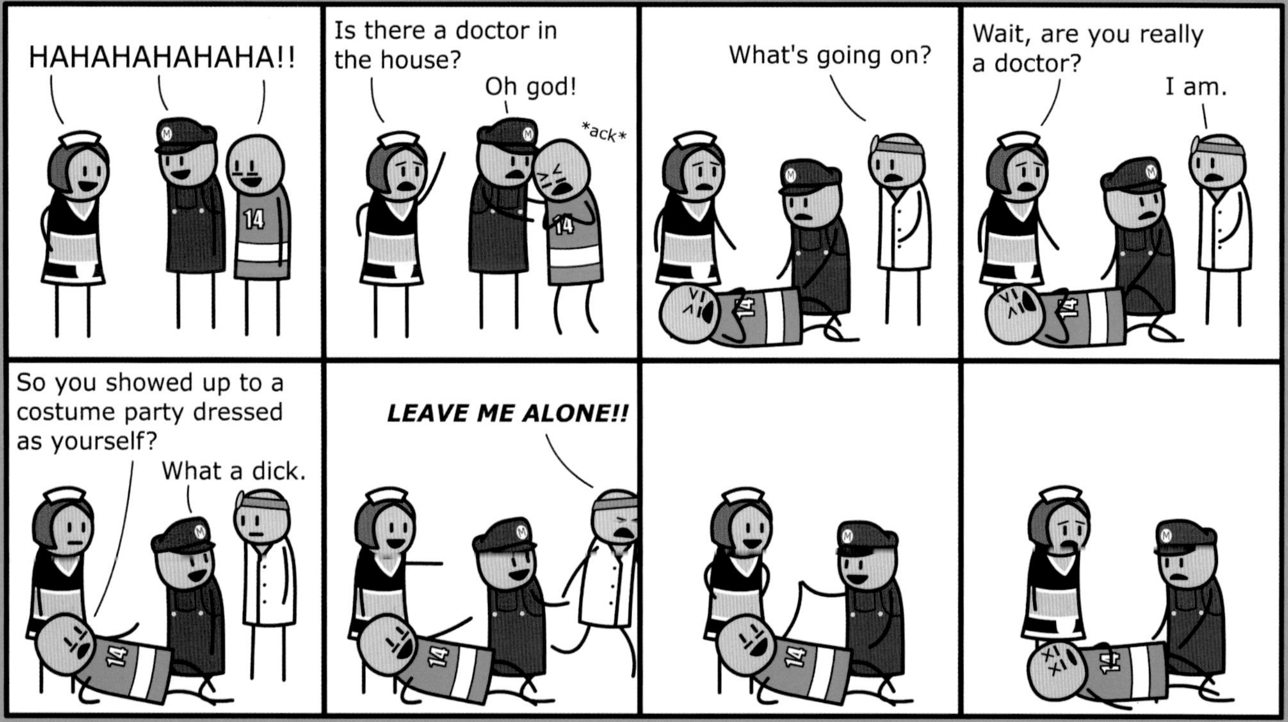
HAHAHAHAHAHA!!
Is there a doctor in the house?
Oh god!
ack
What's going on?
Wait, are you really a doctor?
I am.
So you showed up to a costume party dressed as yourself?
What a dick.
LEAVE ME ALONE!!

...and I guess I've hated ketchup ever since.
Speaking of which, we need to *catch up* on some work soon.
Heh, nice segue.
THANKS!

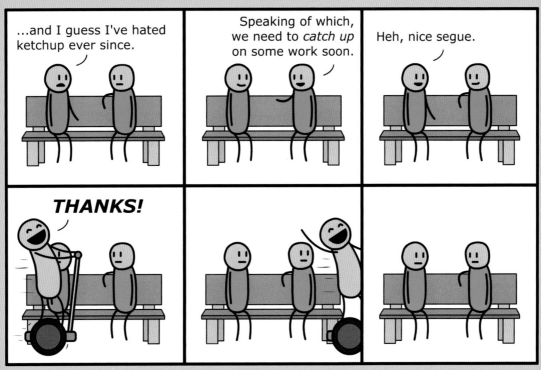

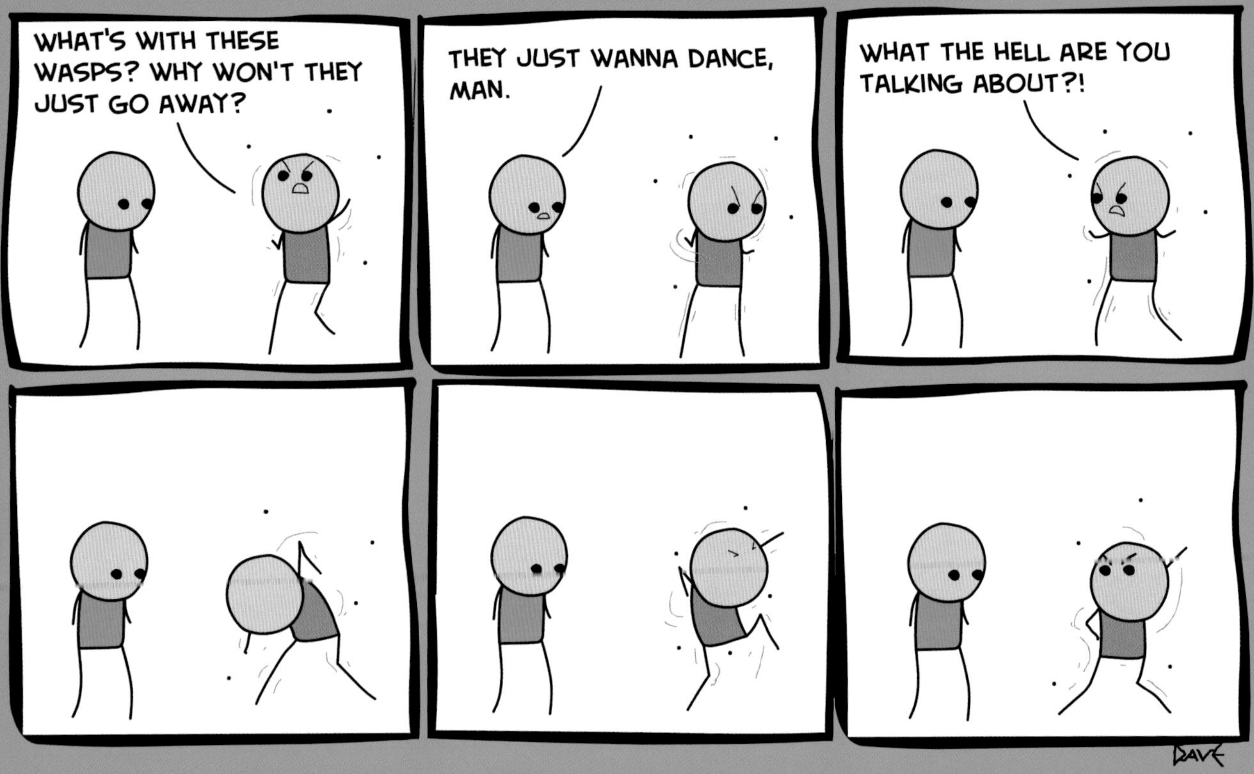
WHAT'S WITH THESE WASPS? WHY WON'T THEY JUST GO AWAY?
THEY JUST WANNA DANCE, MAN.
WHAT THE HELL ARE YOU TALKING ABOUT?!
DAVE

OH GOD LOOK! LIGHTNING JUST STRUCK MY HOUSE!!
HEY DON'T WORRY, LIGHTNING NEVER STRIKES IN THE SAME PLACE TWICE.
HAH, SEE? LOOK!
IT GOT YOUR WIFE THIS TIME!
DAVE

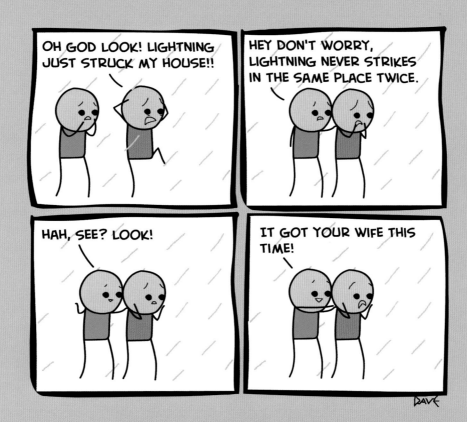

BRUCEWORKS JUST FILED FOR BANKRUPTCY! OUR MERGER'S A BUST!

DAMNIT, JOHNSON! DON'T GIVE ME PROBLEMS. GIVE ME *SOLUTIONS!!*

THEY'RE LIQUIDATING IN A WEEK, AND WE'RE GOING DOWN WITH THEM. SIR, THERE'S... NOTHING WE CAN DO.

I SAY WE CUT OUR TIES AND RUN.

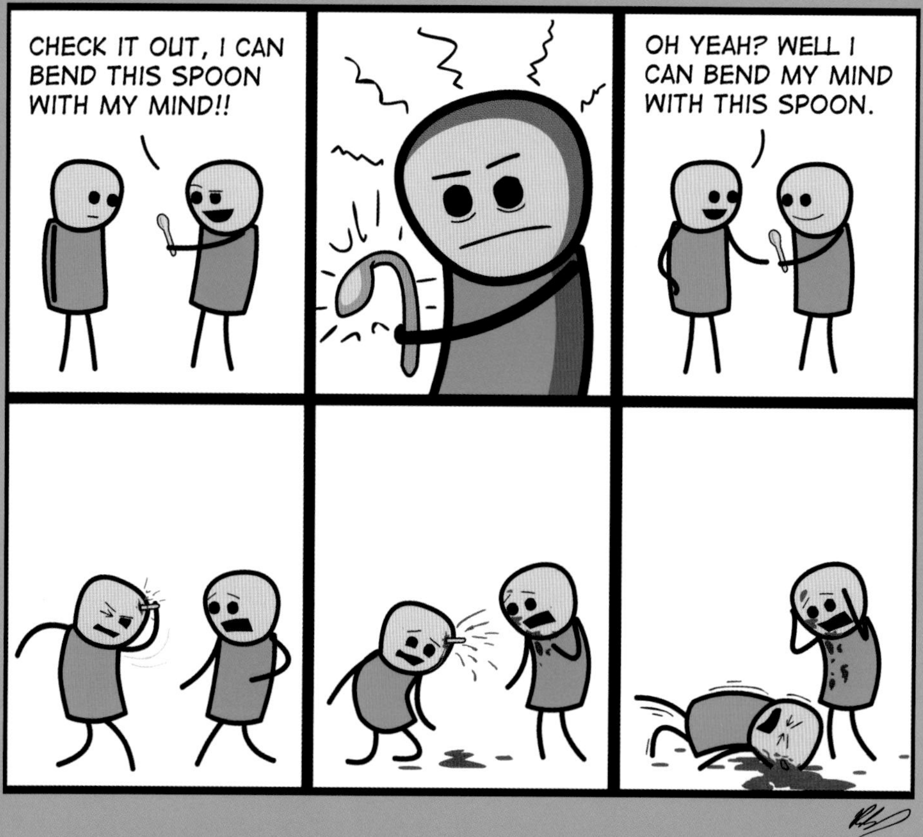
CHECK IT OUT, I CAN BEND THIS SPOON WITH MY MIND!!
OH YEAH? WELL I CAN BEND MY MIND WITH THIS SPOON.

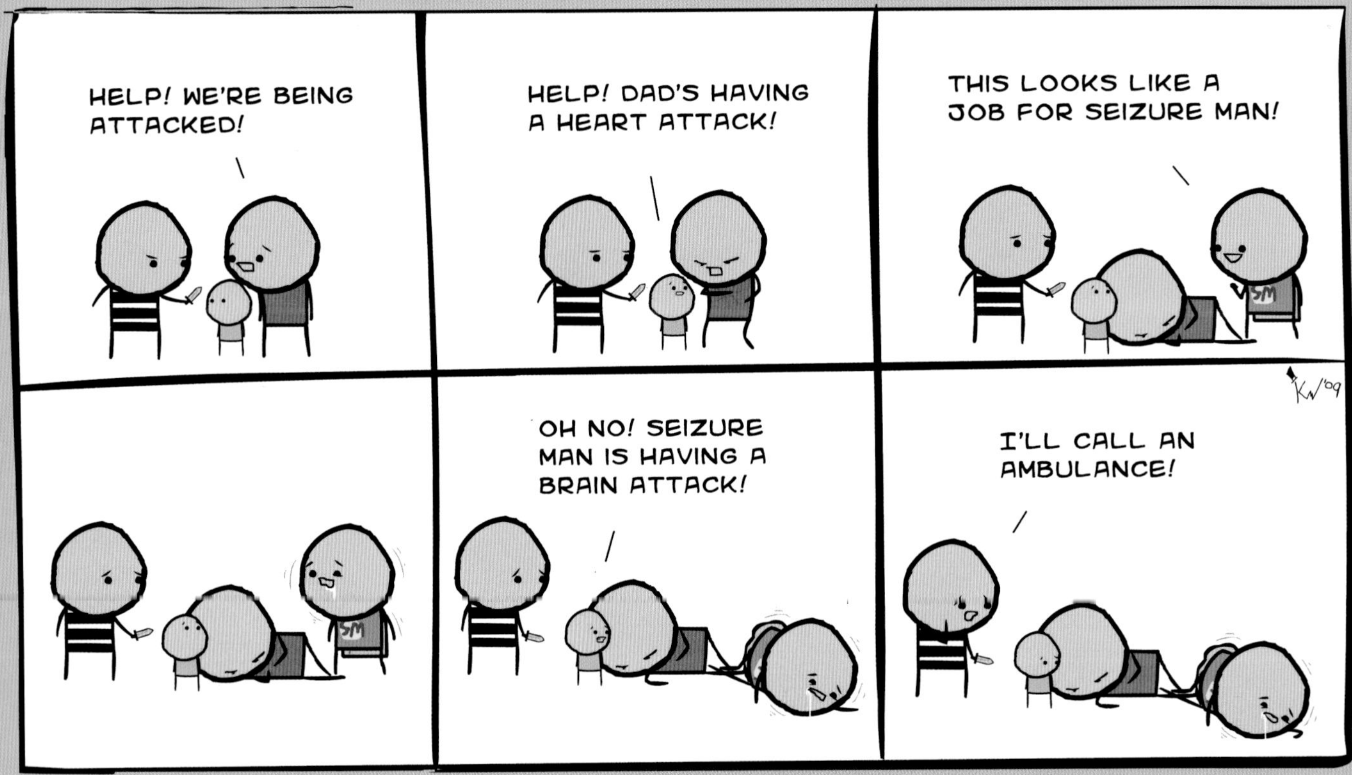
HELP! WE'RE BEING ATTACKED!
HELP! DAD'S HAVING A HEART ATTACK!
THIS LOOKS LIKE A JOB FOR SEIZURE MAN!
SM
SM
OH NO! SEIZURE MAN IS HAVING A BRAIN ATTACK!
I'LL CALL AN AMBULANCE!
KW '09

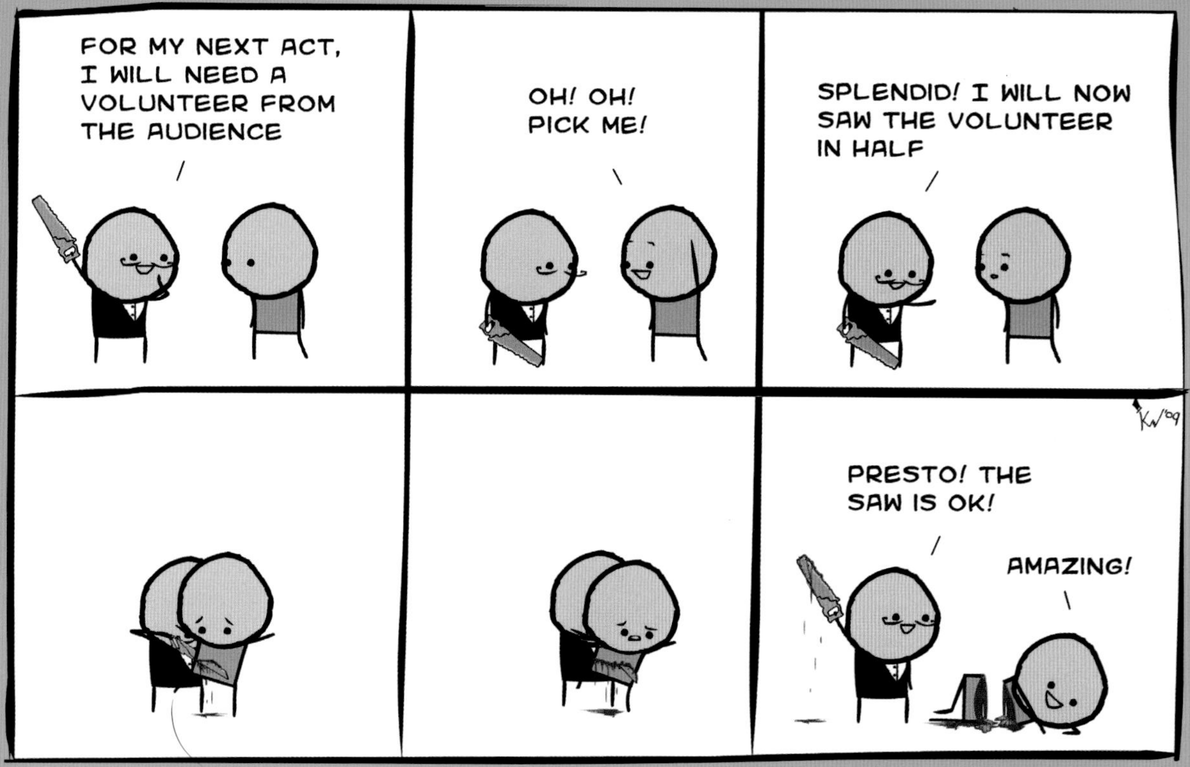
FOR MY NEXT ACT, I WILL NEED A VOLUNTEER FROM THE AUDIENCE
OH! OH! PICK ME!
SPLENDID! I WILL NOW SAW THE VOLUNTEER IN HALF
KW '09
PRESTO! THE SAW IS OK!
AMAZING!

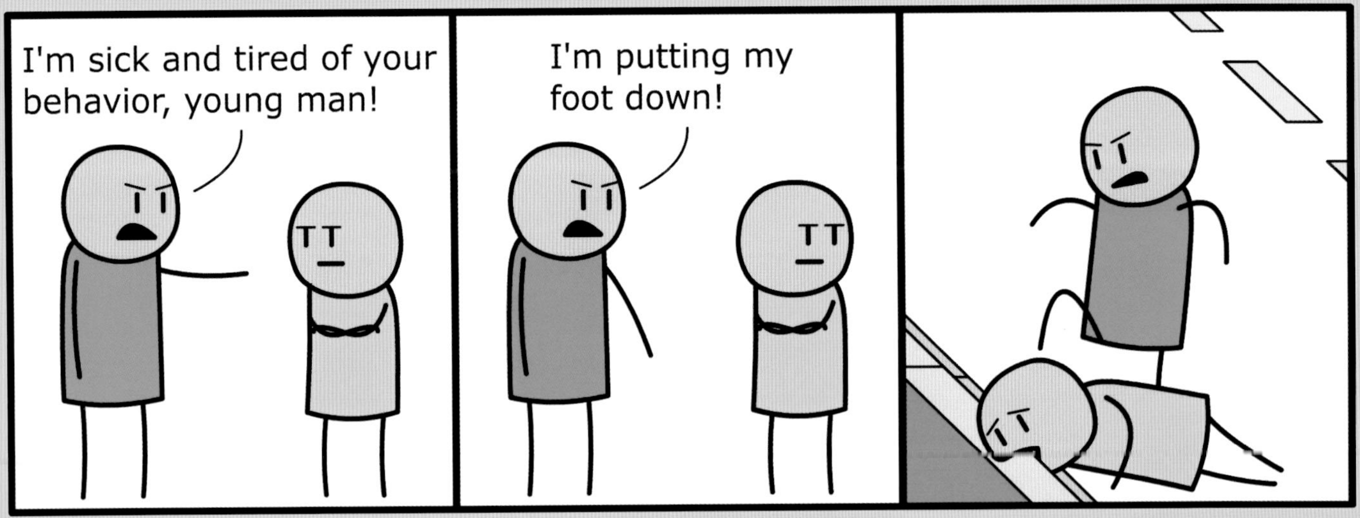
I'm sick and tired of your behavior, young man!
I'm putting my foot down!

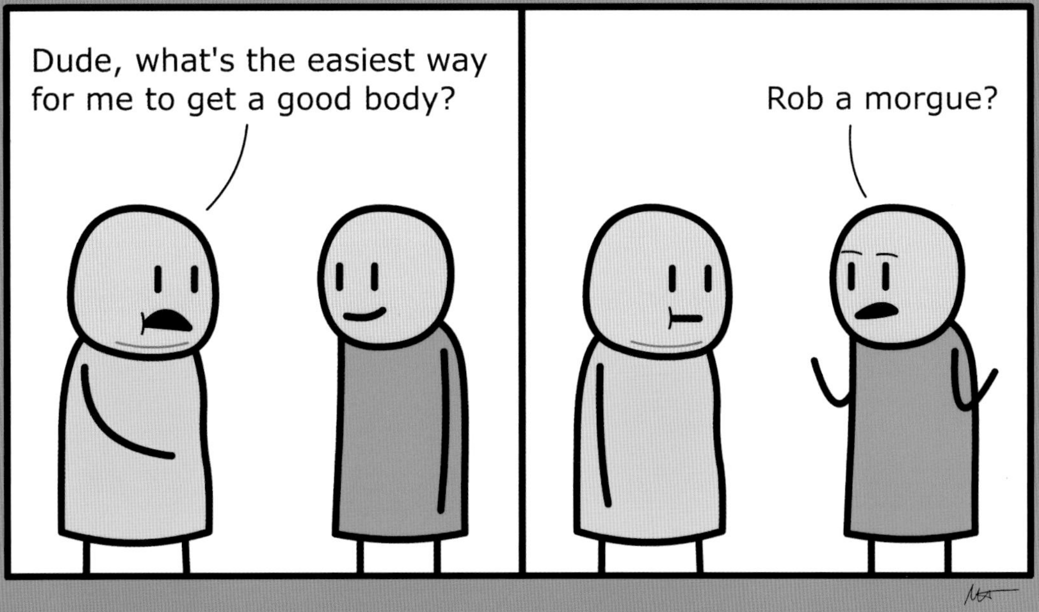
Dude, what's the easiest way for me to get a good body?
Rob a morgue?

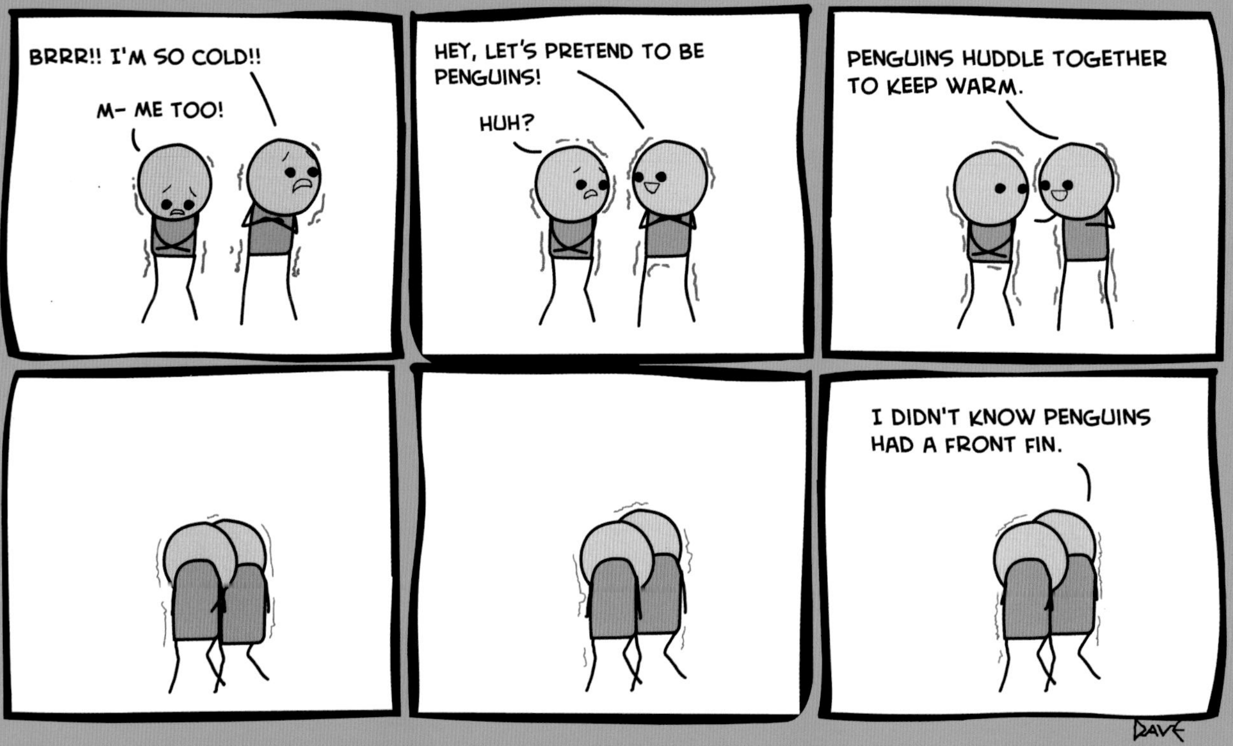
BRRR!! I'M SO COLD!!
M- ME TOO!
HEY, LET'S PRETEND TO BE PENGUINS!
HUH?
PENGUINS HUDDLE TOGETHER TO KEEP WARM.
I DIDN'T KNOW PENGUINS HAD A FRONT FIN.
DAVE

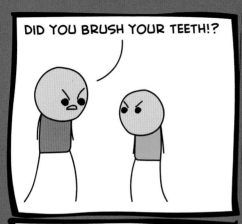

DID YOU BRUSH YOUR TEETH!?

NO!! SCREW YOU, DAD! YOU CAN'T EVER, **EVER** MAKE ME BRUSH MY TEETH!!

DAVE

CHILDISH INSULTS THROUGH THE AGES

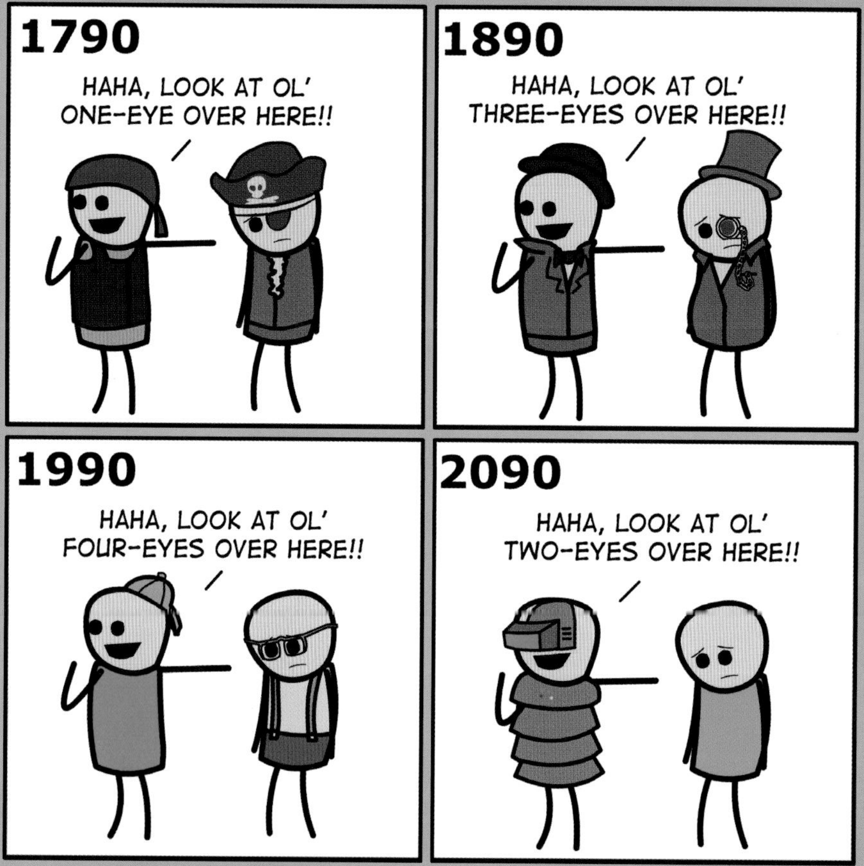
1790
HAHA, LOOK AT OL' ONE-EYE OVER HERE!!
1890
HAHA, LOOK AT OL' THREE-EYES OVER HERE!!
1990
HAHA, LOOK AT OL' FOUR-EYES OVER HERE!!
2090
HAHA, LOOK AT OL' TWO-EYES OVER HERE!!

HONEY, WOULD YOU RATHER HAVE A BOY OR A GIRL?
NEITHER.
YOU DON'T WANT KIDS?
I WANT A HERMAPHRODITE.

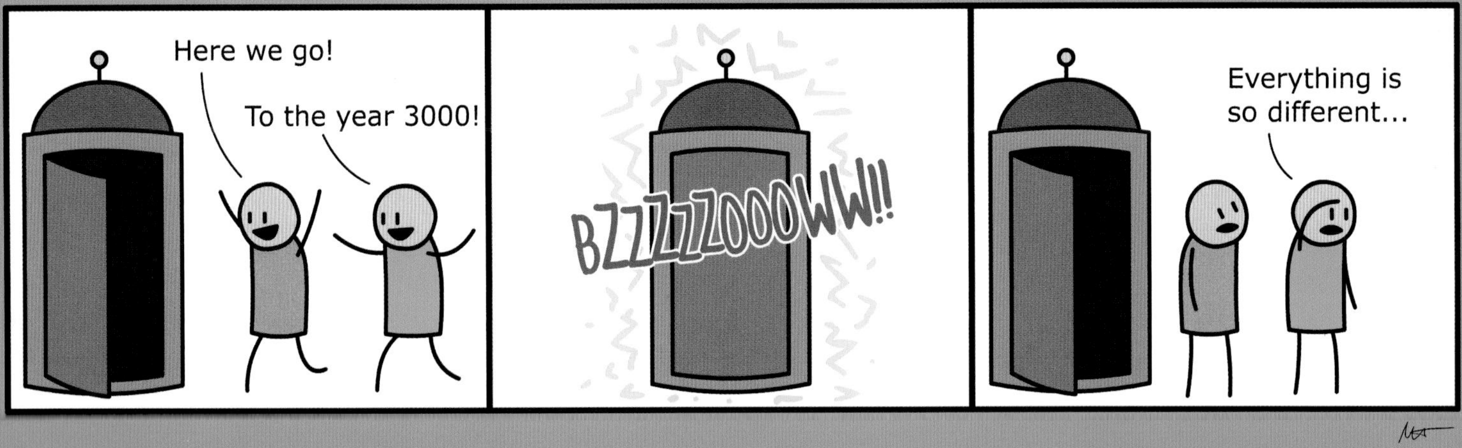
Here we go!
To the year 3000!
BZZZZZZOOOWW!!
Everything is so different...

I KNOW YOU'VE HAD A BAD DAY, SO I WASHED AND FOLDED SOME OF YOUR CLOTHES!
STUPID BITCH!
I CAN'T WEAR THEM FOLDED!

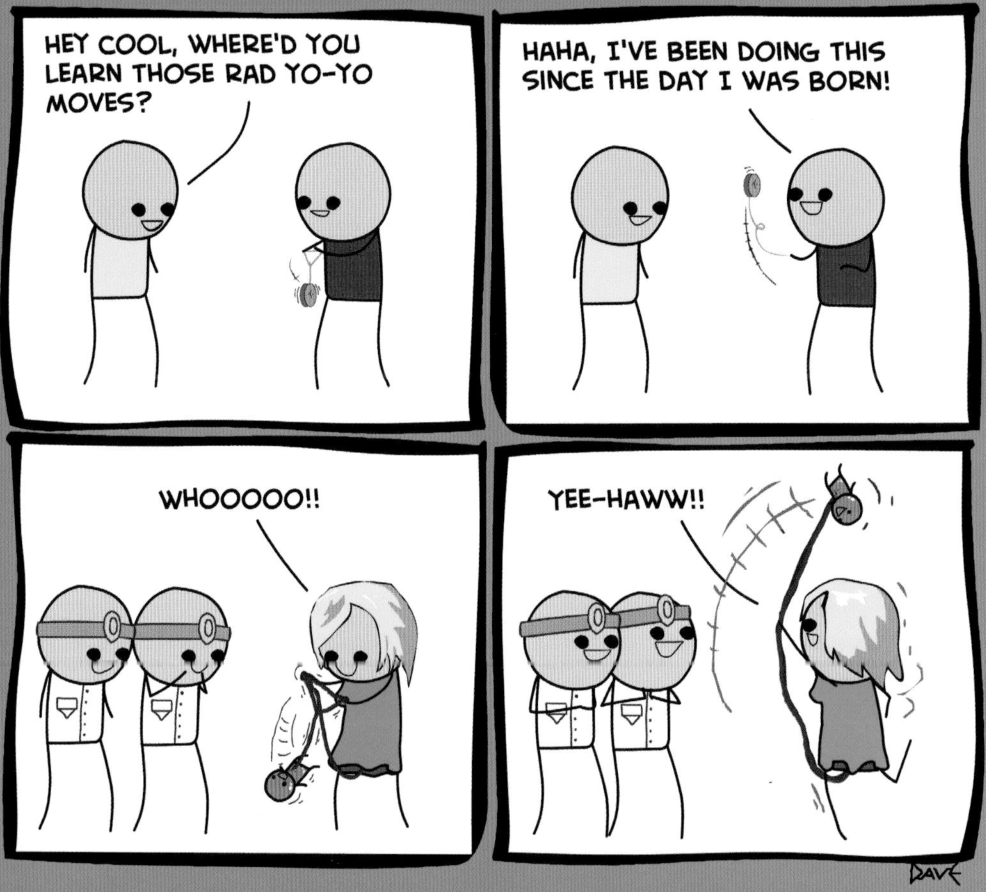
HEY COOL, WHERE'D YOU LEARN THOSE RAD YO-YO MOVES?
HAHA, I'VE BEEN DOING THIS SINCE THE DAY I WAS BORN!
WHOOOOO!!
YEE-HAWW!!
DAVE

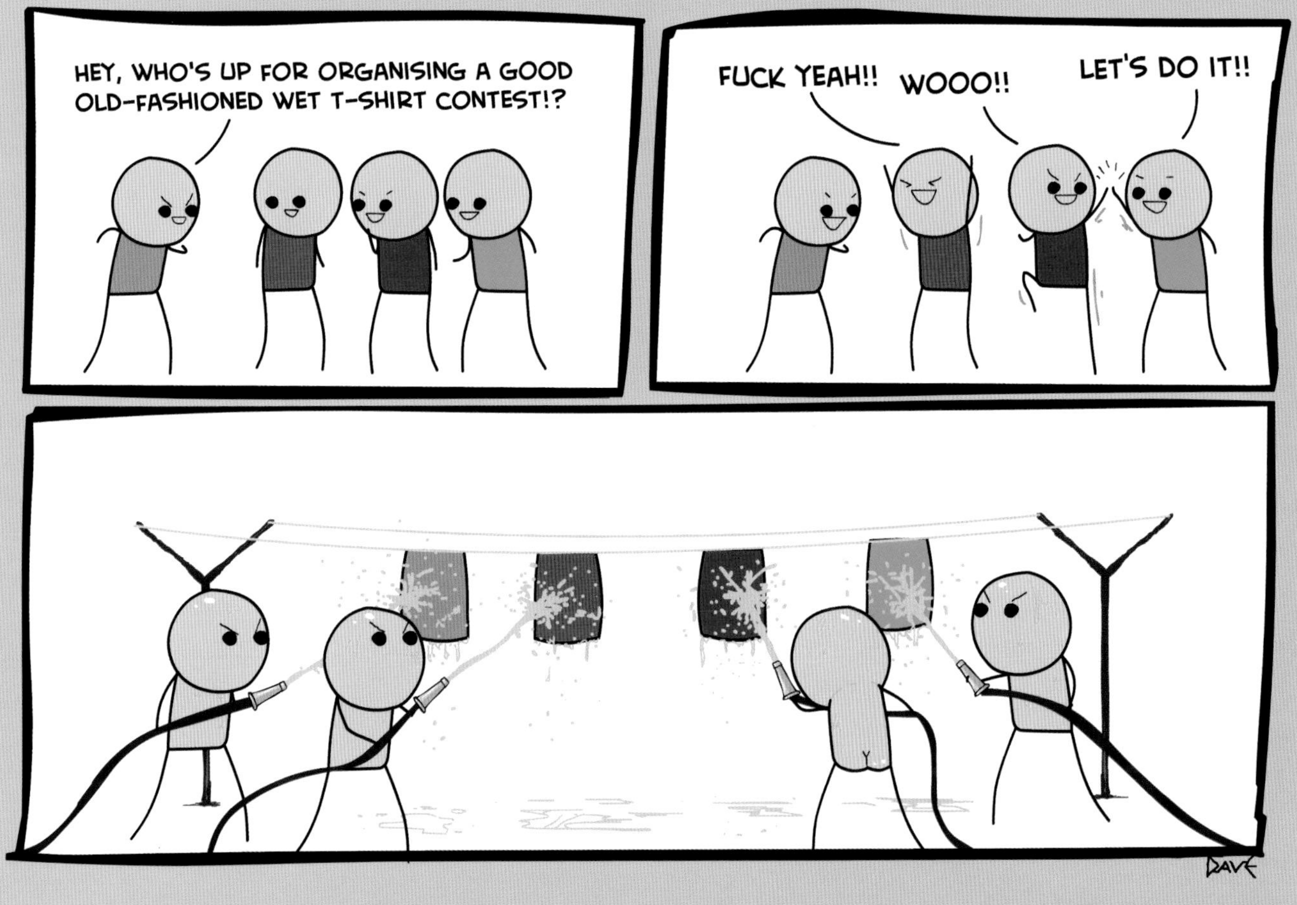
HEY, WHO'S UP FOR ORGANISING A GOOD OLD-FASHIONED WET T-SHIRT CONTEST!?
FUCK YEAH!!
WOOO!!
LET'S DO IT!!
DAVE

ABOUT THE AUTHORS

KRIS

Kris Wilson is a nimble creature, entertaining himself in his natural habitat of Fort Bridger, Wyoming. Growing up in a small town, Kris drew constantly to avoid neurologically damaging boredom. He began drawing Cyanide & Happiness comics at the ripe young age of 16. These early strips were shared with the other dudes and together they developed Cyanide & Happiness into what it is today.

Kris's mild-mannered alter ego enjoys making music, illustrating, painting, swearing, cartwheels, and arson. If you ever see him around, give him all your stuff.

ROB

Rob DenBleyker, the best kisser of the four, hails all the way from Dallas, TX. It's not quite in the heart of Texas, it's more like the left collarbone location-wise. Texas' left, not yours. Rob writes/draws for Cyanide & Happiness, but originally started out doing animation. He still dabbles in it from time to time to help produce animated shorts at Explosm.net.

He joined the Cyanide & Happiness crew just after Kris did, in 2005. He plays cello, piano and people for fools.

MATT

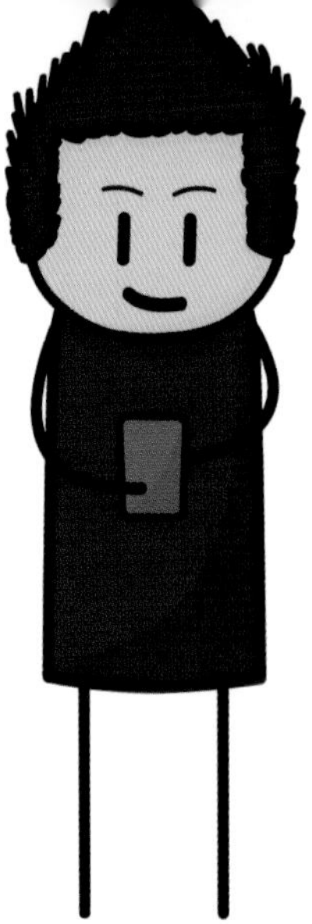

Matt Melvin is a 25-year-old t-shirt aficionado and sideburn enthusiast. When not adding even more filth to the internet, he enjoys criticizing and complaining about movies, listening to music and inventing obscure types of niche sexual acts.

Once a graphic design major, he designed Explosm from the ground up. Thank god that comic thing took off, though. Graphic design is boring as hell. It does have some positive aspects, though. His vast knowledge of the graphic arts obviously lends itself to the rich and deeply detailed stick figures he draws in the comics.

He currently lives in San Diego. He is very tall.

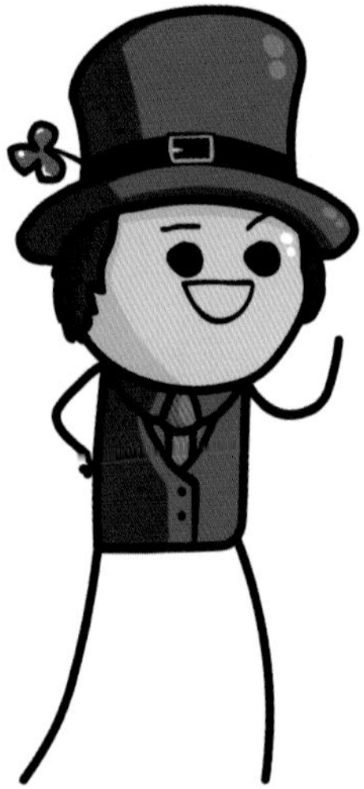

DAVE

Dave McElfatrick is the second oldest of the Explosm team, and therefore statistically the second earliest to die. Dave, unlike the other Explosm guys, hails not from America but from the small town of Coleraine in Northern Ireland. As a result, he has a stupid accent and likes to drink copious amounts of beer. He is currently living in the fair city of Belfast, where he writes and draws for Cyanide & Happiness.

When not indulging his keen interest in animation and animated film (an interest evident in his work with the Cyanide & Happiness animated cartoons), Dave enjoys writing bad music, passing judgement on other bad music, playing guitar badly, illustrating badly, and taking in the local scenery (badly). It's usually quite blurry from the night before. He has two little dogs. They're really cute.

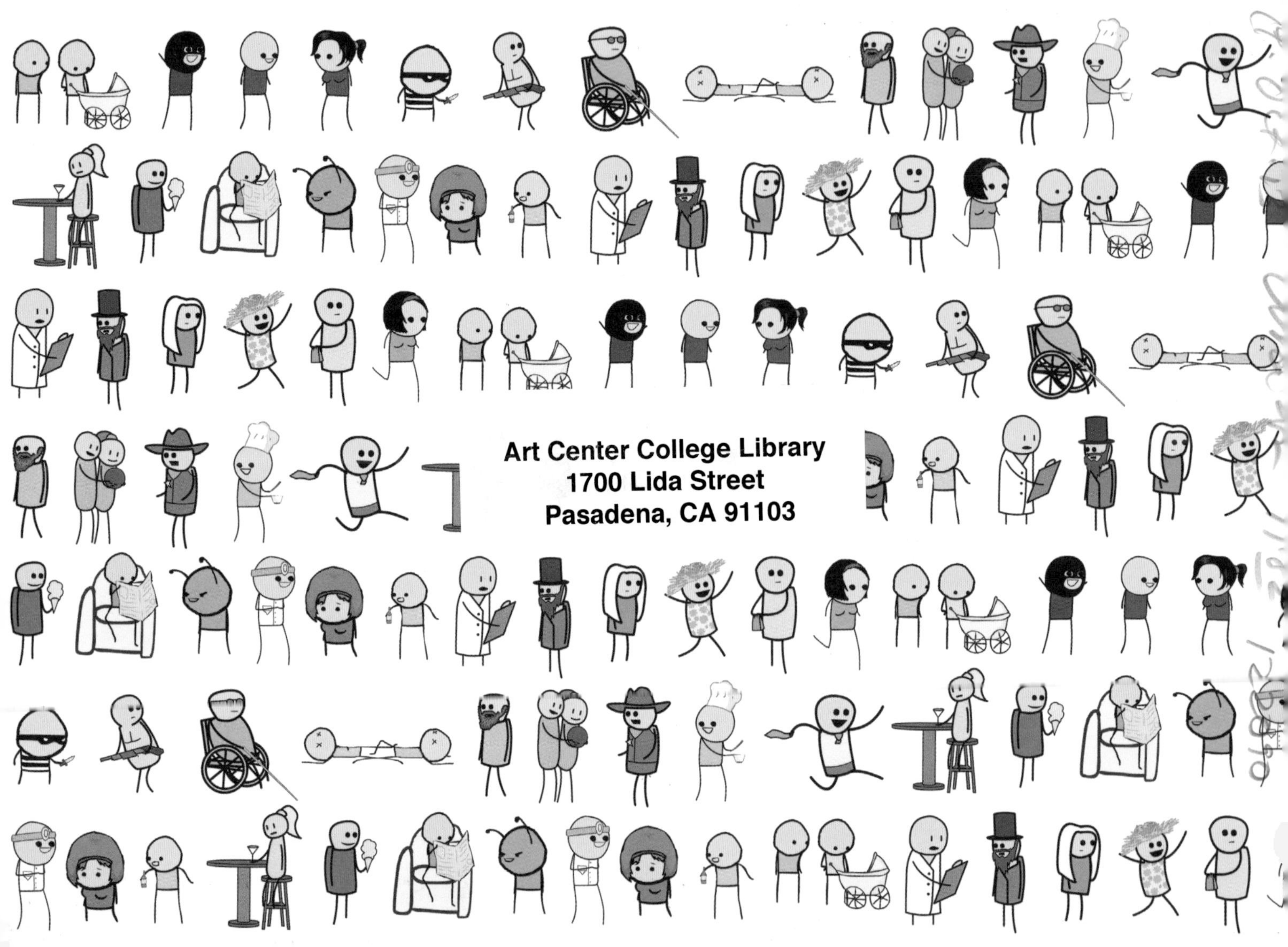